How to read a balance sheet

How to read a balance sheet

SECOND (REVISED) EDITION

International Labour Office   Geneva

ISBN 92-2-103898-X

First published 1966
Fifteenth impression 1984
Second (revised) edition 1985

For permission to use copyright material in the preface and the glossary, grateful acknowledgement is due to Hodder and Stoughton Ltd., publishers of *Accounting reports* (London, 1970) by R. G. A. Boland and D. J. Hall.

Printed in Switzerland

CONTENTS

PREFACE TO THE SECOND (REVISED) EDITION

Accounting has been called the language of business. The balance sheet and the associated financial reports are the principal devices for presenting information about the financial position of a private or public enterprise. Training in accounting and financial management has therefore had a prominent place in the Management Development Programme of the International Labour Office (ILO) since the 1960s, when the first edition of this book was published. The book quickly became a very popular training and self-development text, translated into more than 20 languages and used in over 90 countries.

The revised version of this programmed manual retains the essential structure of the original text but includes several innovations to broaden the scope of the programme, such as:

- new material on the profit and loss account and the sources and uses of funds statement;
- a technical note on inflation accounting;
- a glossary of technical terms;
- shorter chapters with summaries;
- a final quiz to measure the knowledge acquired.

Purpose of the book

Although balance sheets are used throughout the world, their form and the terms used in them vary from place to place according to national and local customs and law. Furthermore, the interpretation of balance sheets is directly related to the associated financial reports such as the profit and loss account, the sources and uses of funds statement, the auditor's certificate and the notes to the financial statements.

The subject is presented here in such a way that even people with limited time for personal study will be able to master it easily. The programme introduces the structure and language of a balance sheet (and of the associated financial reports) and describes how the information given in the various financial reports can be used to assess the financial position of an enterprise. It also illustrates the structure of the resources of an enterprise and explains the enterprise's responsibilities to, and relations with, owners and other bodies.

Accountants, managers, directors, chairmen and shareholders in public and private companies need to be able to interpret financial reports, as do private investors, students of accounting, trade union officials, and many persons concerned with the operation and supervision of public affairs at the local or national level. The growing emphasis on broad consultation and on the popular understanding of development planning may well extend the range of persons to whom such knowledge is useful, especially now that enlightened enterprises in many countries provide a considerable amount of information to their employees and to the community.

Thus, this programmed text can be of use to a wide variety of readers. It has been used with considerable success:

— in commercial colleges and schools;
— in the initial training of industrial, commercial and professional accountants;
— in accounting and financial training for non-financial managers, administrators, scientists, engineers, members of trade unions, and others;
— in the training of management consultants;
— for individual study of basic accounting concepts;
— for group study (the programme is most efficient and effective when learners help and motivate one another in pairs or in small groups).

Accounting language

Like any language, the language of accounting can never express our thoughts with absolute precision and clarity. This language is complex and many of the words used do not mean the same as they do in everyday life. We must learn to think of the accounting, rather than the popular, meaning of such words.

Uncertainty

Accounting encompasses those facts about a business that can be expressed in monetary terms. However, many important business facts, such as the health of the management, the morale of the workers, the state of the market, and so on, cannot be expressed in financial terms. Accounting therefore provides only a *limited picture* of a business.

Accounting figures are thus only professional estimates, *not* scientific facts. The key accounting concept is *materiality*, whereby financial management concentrates on significant (material) values, with relatively little attention to small amounts and small errors.

Conservatism

The practice of accounting arose from practical business activities over a long period of time. In order not to mislead the managers of enterprises (and in order to prevent them from having to pay more income tax than absolutely necessary), accountants tended to be ultra-conservative and to understate rather than overstate the financial position of a business.

Accounting practices, therefore, aim to take profits only when they are reasonably certain and yet, by contrast, to provide for losses as soon as they are known or anticipated. An attitude of *conservatism*, however, could lead to mis-statement of the financial position of a business; hence, generally accepted accounting standards try to present a "true and fair view" of a business.

Consistency and comparability

The basis of all profit is the accounting period during which the profit is realised. Thus 10,000 units for a week is not the same as 10,000 units for the whole year. Accounting figures are not significant in themselves but only when they are compared with other figures for similar periods. The accountant, therefore, despite the problems of uncertainty and conservatism, tries to be *consistent* in his judgement so that the figures he produces are *comparable* from one period to another.

Accounting and auditing standards

Generally accepted *accounting standards* are the concepts used to convert accounting records into reliable accounting reports. In any country such standards may arise from:
–   the professional accounting associations;
–   the legal establishment of an accounting plan *(plan comptable)*, especially in French-speaking countries, which sets out the required accounting records, concepts and reports;
–   income tax laws which may require different accounting concepts for tax purposes; thus the balance sheet for income tax purposes (which is often the published balance sheet) may show a highly conservative (understated) view of the financial position of the business enterprise. Is this "true and fair"?

Similarly, generally accepted *auditing standards* are used for the professional audit of accounting reports so that an "independent" professional auditor may give a "clear" certificate. His certificate generally states that the reports are prepared in accordance with "generally accepted accounting standards" and verified in accordance with "generally accepted auditing standards" to show a "true and fair view" of the business enterprise.

Efforts to achieve internationally acceptable accounting and auditing standards are seriously handicapped by variations in economic, political and legal environments, and by differing objectives for accounting in various countries.

Acknowledgements

The original version of this book was prepared by J. J. H. Halsall, FCA, formerly of the ILO Management Development Branch, who was responsible for the accounting aspects of the text in association with Learning Systems Ltd. In 1984 the book was extensively revised and rewritten by Robert G. A. Boland, FCA, Ph.D., of the ILO Management Development Branch, assisted by Richard Oxtoby, Ph.D., and Catherine d'Arcangues, Ph.D., consultants.

Many accounting and management development professionals working with the ILO Management Development Programme have helped us by providing useful comments and testing the manual. Without their contribution, the publication and wide application of this manual would not have been possible.

TECHNICAL DATA

Type of programme

Linear – that is, the programme is to be done set by set and chapter by chapter. Difficulties should be resolved by repeating the sets and by using the glossary.

Estimated completion time

While you will work at your own pace, the results of our pilot tests indicate that most people complete this programme (including the mini-tests and the final quiz) in eight to 16 hours.

Testing

The original programme was extensively field-tested by members of the target population in various countries and regions with satisfactory results. However, the International Labour Office would welcome further reports from users who have worked through this revised edition.

Appendices

The technical note on inflation accounting contained in Appendix A may be useful to students for reference at a later stage. A glossary of some of the accounting terms used in different parts of the world is to be found in Appendix B at the end of the book. Students may like to make their own additions to the glossary as they come across further accounting terms and alternative expressions.

Presentation of balance sheets

The presentation of figures on balance sheets and on other financial statements varies from one enterprise to another. On the balance sheets in this book, amounts over 999 are presented without a comma, but in the text itself a comma is inserted.

Suggested uses for the programme

The programme can be used:
(*a*) for individual study;
(*b*) as a back-up to training in management and accounting centres;
(*c*) for group study – the programme is most effective when learners help and motivate one another in pairs or in small groups.

HOW THE PROGRAMME WORKS

1. Tear off the flap at the front of the book and use it as a mask to cover the left-hand column of this page.

2. Read Frame A carefully and write the missing word in the last column.

3. Move the mask down and check your answer.

4. Then read Frame B and write the missing words in the right-hand column, and so on.

5. Whenever you turn a page, mask the whole column at once and slide the mask down only *after* you have written your answer in the last column.

CHECK	FRAME	YOUR ANSWER
Is your answer right? Check below.	**A.** In this programme you will often be asked to fill in missing words as you go along. Sometimes you have to write one word, and sometimes more than one. Where there is one dash you write _____ word.	
A one	**B.** Where there is one dash you write one word. Where there are two dashes you write _____ _____. Sometimes these two dashes may be joined by a hyphen to indicate a hyphenated word.	
B two words	**C.** Just occasionally you will have to fill in more than two words. In this case there will be a row of dots. Where there is a row of dots you write	

CHECK	FRAME	YOUR ANSWER
C more than two words	**D.** Going back for a minute: one dash calls for _____ word; two dashes call for _____ _____; and a row of dots means that you have to fill in	
D one two words more than two words	**E.** When square brackets containing two or three words or phrases are separated by oblique strokes, you should select the right word or phrase. For example: This book is [a conventional textbook/a new type of textbook].	
E a new type of textbook	**F.** When several alternatives are given in the following way: (*a*) this sentence contains four words; (*b*) this sentence contains five words; (*c*) this sentence contains six words; you should choose the correct alternative and write (*a*), (*b*) or (*c*) in the answer column.	
F (*b*)	**G.** Before you start on the programme itself, note that you don't have to guess to get the right answers. Read the frames carefully and they will give you the information which you need to get the r_____ answers. In this case the "r" before the dash means that the missing word which you have to fill in begins with an "r".	
G right	**H.** Don't hesitate to write a word because you think that it is too simple or obvious. The whole idea of this programme is that it moves in easy steps. You never have to g_____ the answers.	

CHECK	FRAME	YOUR ANSWER
H guess	**I.** A reminder: Where one word is wanted there will be _____ dash. Two dashes mean that you should write _____ _____. A row of dots means that you should write	
I one two words more than two words	**J.** Where there are square brackets containing two or three words or phrases, you should [choose the correct word or phrase/simply read them].	
J choose the correct word or phrase	**K.** When several alternatives are given: (*a*) copy the whole sentence; (*b*) choose the incorrect alternative; (*c*) choose the correct alternative; choose the correct alternative and write (*a*), (*b*) or (*c*) in the answer column.	
K (*c*)	**L.** Finally, the correct way to go through the programme is: (*a*) read the frame and fill in the missing _____ word, _____ _____, or ...., or choose the [correct/incorrect] word or phrase; (*b*) move the mask down so that you can read the r_____ answer, (*c*) go on to the next f_____	
L (*a*) one two words more than two words correct (*b*) right (*c*) frame	Now start working through the programme itself. Read each frame carefully before writing anything. On turning over each page, remember to cover up the left-hand column with the mask before going on to the next frame.	

IMPORTANT NOTE

Read each frame carefully. If you do not understand something the first time, read the frame again before going to the next one. Do not spend too much time on any one frame; the programme deliberately repeats all the key points to be learned.

Do not hesitate to repeat the frames and answers aloud if it helps you to learn better. Try to work quickly and repeat a whole set again if you feel uncertain. Use the glossary for difficult technical terms.

Go on steadily set by set and never start a new set when you are tired. Do not try to do too much in one sitting but make time available to finish the whole programme over a few days; repeat it as necessary.

Working in pairs or in small groups is recommended; it makes the work more interesting and improves the quality of the learning.

PROGRESS WORK SHEET

Chapter/Set		Estimated time [1] (minutes)	Actual time (minutes)	Total frames	Frames right	Frames wrong
Chapter 1	Set 1	10		20		
	Set 2	15		25		
	Study glossary	–		–		
Chapter 2	Set 3	25		50		
	Set 4	25		50		
	Mini-test	20		20		
Chapter 3	Set 5	20		39		
	Set 6	15		35		
	Set 7	15		30		
	Mini-test	20		20		
Chapter 4	Set 8	30		64		
	Set 9	20		45		
	Mini-test	20		20		
Chapter 5	Set 10	25		40		
	Set 11	20		41		
	Mini-test	15		20		
Chapter 6	Set 12	20		40		
	Set 13	20		50		
	Set 14	10		15		
	Mini-test	20		20		
Chapter 7	Set 15	25		52		
	Set 16	20		22		
	Mini-test	10		10		
Final quiz		50		60		
Totals		470		788		

[1] If your English is not fluent, you may need to add up to 100 per cent to each of the estimated times.

INTRODUCTION   I

1. SET 1. SOME ASPECTS OF ACCOUNTING

Estimated time: 10 minutes

Summary

There is no set of detailed rules that is universally agreed upon for drawing
up the financial statements of a business enterprise. As a result, balance
sheets of different business enterprises (especially if they are from
different countries) may differ in detail from each other. The basic
principles are always the same, however, and all balance sheets have
something in common.

Accountants drawing up balance sheets are sometimes required to
make judgements about monetary values. The *criteria* they choose are
important, but it is even more vital that the accountants should be
consistent in using them.

Accounting figures are not significant in themselves. They are significant
only when *compared* with other similar sets of figures. The significance
(or materiality) of accounting figures depends very much on the date or
time period to which they refer.

To be useful and reliable, financial statements should be timely and should
be professionally audited.

IMPORTANT NOTE

At the start of each set there is a summary (as above) of the
technical terms and ideas to be learned from the set.

If you already understand all of the summary, do not complete the
set, but pass on to the next one.

If you do not completely understand every technical term and idea
in the summary, do the whole set. Do not attempt to do only parts
of a particular set.

CHECK	FRAME	YOUR ANSWER

(Don't forget to cover up the left-hand column of each page with your mask and to move the mask down to check your answer before going on to the next frame.)

Is your answer right? Check below.

1. Balance sheets are produced by accountants. Before we start to look at the _____ sheet itself, let us look at a few general features of accounting practice which should be borne in mind as you work through this book.

1
balance

2. Accountants have different opinions on many subjects – within the field of accounting as well as outside it. So it is not surprising that there are some variations in _____ practice to be found in different countries, in different parts of the same country, and even between different _____ working in the same place at the same time.

2
accounting
accountants

3. This means that there is no single, universally accepted form for the presentation of those financial statements which an accountant produces to describe the financial situation of a b_____ enterprise. Individual differences among accountants result in different forms of presentation of _____ statements.

3
business
financial

4. Despite these d_____, there are some basic principles which are generally accepted. By the time you have finished working through this book, you should have a good knowledge of these basic principles.

CHECK	FRAME	YOUR ANSWER

CHECK

4
differences

5
principles

6
sheet

7
accountant

8
decreased
value

FRAME

5. However, don't be surprised if you come across a balance sheet some time which does not look exactly like those you will see in this book. Different balance sheets may differ in the detail of their presentation, but they all follow the same basic _____.

6. One reason for the differences in accounting practice is that it is difficult to assess accurately some of the monetary values which appear on the balance sheet. A balance _____ appears to be a very "definite" statement about various sums of money.

7. This apparently "definite" statement may, however, be deceptive. Many of the figures appearing on a balance sheet are estimated by the a_____.

8. For example, what is the value today of the land and buildings which a business enterprise bought 50 years ago? The land may well have increased in value but the value of the buildings has probably d_____ as a result of decay and the wear and tear of 50 years of use. The accountant must decide what _____ to put on them on the balance sheet.

9. Or take the example of a business enterprise which buys goods for resale. When does it actually make a profit on a particular item: when it receives the item into stock, when it receives the customer's order for that item, when it dispatches the item to the customer, or when the customer finally pays the account? Again, there is uncertainty and the _____ has to make a judgement.

CHECK	FRAME	YOUR ANSWER

9
accountant

10. Most of these judgements are made in terms of generally accepted accounting practices, as you will see later in this book. Bear in mind, however, that many of the apparently precise figures appearing on a ＿＿＿ ＿＿＿ are estimates made by the accountant who drew it up and that different accounting ＿＿＿ may be followed in different parts of the world and at different times.

10
balance sheet
practices

11. However, the particular criteria an accountant uses in making a judgement are not so important as the need for the accountant to be consistent in using the same c＿＿＿ on different occasions.

11
criteria

12. Accounting figures are not significant in themselves. They are only significant when compared with other ＿＿＿ for a similar previous period, for a budget estimate, or even for another business enterprise.

12
figures

13. Accountants therefore, despite the problem of uncertainty, try to be ＿＿＿ in their judgement, so that the figures they produce are comparable from one period to another.

13
consistent

14. Another point we need to consider in this introduction is the importance of time periods and dates in assessing the significance of the information contained in f＿＿＿ statements.

CHECK	FRAME	YOUR ANSWER

14
financial

15. Sometimes the financial position of a business enterprise changes dramatically in a very short space of _____. The position on June 30 may be very different from what it was on January 1.

15
time

16. Again, a certain sum of money may represent a very significant (material) profit if it was made over one month, but may represent a very poor profit for one whole year. In assessing the significance (materiality) of the figures contained in a balance sheet or in any other financial statement, it is essential to know the _____ period or _____ to which they refer. Incidentally, what kind of chair would be a "material" asset? ....

16
time
date
An antique chair
which is of
significant value

17. Financial statements describe the financial situation of a business enterprise over time. They are used by the different parties who have relations with the enterprise, including management, trade unions, government, creditors, banks and shareholders. To be useful, the statements should contain up-to-date information; they must therefore be [timely/delayed].

17
timely

18. To be useful, financial statements should be:

(*a*) timely and reasonably accurate;

(*b*) absolutely accurate, no matter how late;

(*c*) delayed for as long as possible.

CHECK	FRAME	YOUR ANSWER

18
(a)

19. Most financial statements cover a period of one year – so how soon after the end of the year do you think they should be available in order to be "timely"?

(a) within 3 months;

(b) 4 to 6 months;

(c) 7 to 12 months;

(d) 13 to 48 months.

19
(a)

20. Now, financial statements may also be submitted to an auditor for an independent professional opinion on the judgements made by the accountant. Are such audited reports more reliable? _____.

20
Yes

You have now reached the end of the general introduction. Note how long you took to complete this set and the number of wrong answers you gave. Enter these on the Progress Work Sheet on page XVII. Then turn to the summary at the beginning of this set and read it through again before moving on to Set 2.

I. SET 2. WHAT IS A BALANCE SHEET?

Estimated time: 15 minutes

Summary

A balance sheet is a statement of those assets and liabilities of a business enterprise that can be given a value in terms of money; it shows both the assets and how the assets are financed; the figures are estimates, not scientific facts.

The liabilities indicate what money has been made available to the enterprise, and from where.

The assets show how the enterprise has used the money made available to it.

Total assets must always equal total liabilities to creditors and shareholders.

Every balance sheet must include the name of the enterprise and the date to which the figures in the balance sheet refer.

The balance sheet is one of the financial statements of a company and needs to be supported by:
(*a*) the profit and loss account (income statement);
(*b*) the sources and uses of funds statement (funds flow statement);
(*c*) notes to the financial statements;
(*d*) the auditor's certificate.

CHECK	FRAME	YOUR ANSWER

Is your answer
right? Check below.

1. A balance sheet may look rather complicated but basically it is a simple statement about a business enterprise.

Most business enterprises produce statements at regular intervals showing what they own and what they owe.

A balance sheet is a statement of what an enterprise _____ and what it _____ at a particular date.

I
owns
owes

2. The things that a business enterprise owns are called its assets.

The various sums of money that a business enterprise owes are called its liabilities.

Would a company's buildings and manufacturing tools be classed as assets or as liabilities? _____.

2
Assets

3. Assets include land, buildings, manufacturing equipment, motor vehicles, fixtures and fittings and anything else an enterprise o_____ that can be given a value in terms of money.

Can the stocks of raw materials held by a manufacturing company be given a value in monetary terms? _____.

3
owns
Yes

4. Stocks of raw materials (and finished products) are things owned by an enterprise that can be given a value in _____ terms. They are classed as _____.

CHECK	FRAME	YOUR ANSWER
4 monetary assets	**5.** Now, to acquire its assets, an enterprise must obtain money from various sources; for instance, it may borrow from loan companies or from banks. It then o_____ this money.	
5 owes	**6.** The various amounts of money owed by an enterprise are called its _____.	
6 liabilities	**7.** As well as borrowing from banks and other sources, many companies obtain a good deal of the money that they need from their shareholders. The shareholders of a company generally subscribe, or make money available, for the life of the _____.	
7 company	**8.** Such money is known as shareholders' funds, and is subscribed for the life of the company; it will be repaid to the shareholders only if the company is wound up. Nevertheless, the money is still o_____ to the shareholders.	
8 owed	**9.** The money that is subscribed by shareholders is in fact _____ to the shareholders, and it is therefore part of the company's [assets/liabilities].	
9 owed liabilities	**10.** Balance sheets may be set out in different ways, but however they are set out, they always show the _____ and _____ of the enterprise concerned.	

CHECK	FRAME	YOUR ANSWER

10
assets
liabilities

HANDICRAFTS LTD.
Balance sheet at 31 December 1984
(expressed in "world currency units" (WCU))

ASSETS		LIABILITIES	
Raw materials, etc.	6 920	Bank overdraft	4 300
Land, buildings, etc.	17 500	Long-term mortage loan owed to loan company	14 000
		Money subscribed by shareholders	6 120
Total assets		Total liabilities	

11. Here is a very simple balance sheet. This balance sheet shows the assets and liabilities of _____ _____ (whom?) at

....

(date). Both the assets and the liabilities are expressed in m_____ terms. Fill in the two missing totals on the balance sheet. _____. _____. Are these totals the same or different? _____.

11
Handicrafts Ltd.
31 December 1984
monetary
24,420, 24,420
Same

12. The name "balance sheet" comes from the fact that the total _____ always equal the total _____. In other words, they b_____ each other.

12
assets
liabilities
balance

13. Let us see why the total assets and the total liabilities are in balance. Look at the balance sheet of Handicrafts Ltd. again. The bank, the loan company, and the shareholders have all made money available to the company.

In other words, the [assets/liabilities] on the balance sheet show what money has been made available to the company from various sources.

CHECK	FRAME	YOUR ANSWER

13
liabilities

14. Now, an enterprise obtains money with the object of employing it: for instance, to buy raw materials, etc.

We can see how an enterprise has employed or used its money by looking at the _____ on the balance sheet.

14
assets

15. The liabilities, then, show what _____ has been made available to the enterprise, and the _____ show how this money has been used.

15
money
assets

16. The total assets and the total liabilities will be equal because the _____ show the money that has been made available to the enterprise and the _____ show how this money is employed by the enterprise.

16
liabilities
assets

Balance sheet
(expressed in WCU)

ASSETS		LIABILITIES	
Raw materials, etc.	12 000	Bank overdraft	7 200
Land, buildings, etc.	20 800	Long-term mortage loan owed to loan company	10 000
		Money subscribed by shareholders	15 600
Total assets	32 800	Total liabilities	32 800

17. Here is another simple balance sheet. Look at it carefully and compare it with the one in frame 11.

This new balance sheet has two things missing. These are ....

....

CHECK	FRAME	YOUR ANSWER

17
the name of the
enterprise, and the
date of the balance
sheet

18. If you are looking at a balance sheet in order to assess the current position of a particular enterprise, it is obviously most important to make sure that you have the balance sheet for the right enterprise.

You will also want to know whether you are looking at the most recent balance sheet.

The first two things to look for on a balance sheet, then, are the _____ of the enterprise and the _____ of the balance sheet.

18
name
date

HANDICRAFTS LTD.
Balance sheet at 31 December 1984
(expressed in WCU)

ASSETS		LIABILITIES	
Raw materials, etc.	6 920	Bank overdraft	4 300
Land, buildings, etc.	17 500	Long-term mortage loan owed to loan company	14 000
		Money subscribed by shareholders	6 120
Total assets	24 420	Total liabilities	24 420

19. Now look at the balance sheet that is given above. Does it convey the same information as that given on the balance sheet in frame 11? _____.

19
Yes

20. Balance sheets can be set out in many different ways. But, however they may vary in detail, balance sheets should always include two main groups of figures: the _____ and the _____.

CHECK	FRAME	YOUR ANSWER

20
assets
liabilities

21. It is important to note before finishing this section that many of the factors which affect the position of an enterprise cannot be expressed in monetary terms. For instance, a company might be fortunate in having a highly trained and stable labour force, or some major political change may be coming. Are factors like these indicated on a balance sheet? _____.

21
No
(*Such factors are indicated in the notes to the financial statements.*)

22. Now, we said in the summary that the balance sheet must be associated with other financial statements, such as the profit and loss account, the sources and uses of funds statement, notes to the financial statements and finally the _____ certificate.

22
auditor's

23. If we cannot find the information we need on the balance sheet, the profit and loss account, the sources and uses of funds statement or the auditor's certificate, then the last place to look is in the _____ to the financial statements.

23
notes

24. All of these associated financial statements will be discussed later in the programme. At this stage you must just recognise that the balance sheet alone [is/is not] sufficient.

24
is not

25. Incidentally, is a *very small* antique chair a "material asset"? ....

25
Yes, if it is of significant value!

That is the end of the second set. Note the time you took to complete this set and the number of frames in which you made ▶

CHECK	FRAME	YOUR ANSWER

a mistake, and enter these details on the Progress Work Sheet.

Normally there is a review in the form of a mini-test after each chapter. However, for this chapter you should explore the glossary in Appendix B. Look up "accounting concepts" in the glossary and then find the definition of each concept. Finally, read the summary at the beginning of each set in the chapter once again before going on to the next chapter.

THE INVESTMENT SIDE OF   **2**
THE BALANCE SHEET – ASSETS

2. SET 3. TYPES OF ASSETS AND THEIR LIQUIDITY

Estimated time: 25 minutes

Summary

The assets of a business enterprise are usually listed on a balance sheet in two main groups: fixed and current.

Fixed assets are acquired for long-term use in the enterprise, do not vary greatly from day to day, and are only infrequently converted into cash during the life of the enterprise.

Current assets generally include cash, customers' accounts and inventories that will be converted into cash during the operating cycle of the business; they are likely to vary continually.

Liquidity refers to the ease with which assets can be converted into cash; thus, current assets are more liquid than fixed assets.

Those current assets that can be most quickly converted into cash are known as quick assets.

Panel A at page 20 lists the assets schematically.

CHECK	FRAME	YOUR ANSWER

Is your answer right? Check below	*CURRENT ASSETS AND FIXED ASSETS* **1.** First a reminder: the liabilities on a balance sheet show what money, or finance, has been made available to the enterprise from various sources, and the assets show how this money is _____.	
I employed (*or* used)	**2.** In simpler terms, the assets are what an enterprise o_____, and the liabilities are what it o_____.	
2 owns owes	**3.** Now a company may not only _____ money to others, but may itself be owed money by other people. At any one time it will probably have customers who have not yet paid for goods or services which they have already received.	
3 owe	**4.** Although this money has not yet been received by the company, these "customers' accounts" would always be listed on a balance sheet under the [assets/liabilities].	
4 assets	**5.** What we have referred to here as "customers' accounts" is sometimes referred to as "debtors" or "accounts receivable". Thus, debtors or accounts receivable would appear on the balance sheet under the _____.	
5 assets	The balance sheets in Set 2 gave very short lists of assets. *Panel A* gives an example of the kind of list of assets which you might find on a balance sheet. Before proceeding with frames 6 to 26, open out *Panel A* (page 20). ▶	

CHECK	FRAME	YOUR ANSWER
	6. Assets are usually listed on a balance sheet in two main groups: _____ assets and _____ assets.	
6 current fixed	**7.** Look at the two groups again. One of them is a list of assets which are generally intended for use in the business over a relatively long period. Which would you say are the long-term assets: the current assets or the fixed assets? _____ _____.	
7 Fixed assets	**8.** Assets which are generally intended for use over a long period include land, buildings, ... (give two others). They are called _____ assets.	
8 plant and machinery, motor vehicles, fixtures and fittings (*any two*) fixed	**9.** Look at the two groups of assets again. Which group is *not* likely to vary greatly in quantity from day to day: the current assets or the fixed assets? _____ _____.	
9 Fixed assets	**10.** Fixed assets are acquired for _____-term use in the business. They [are likely/are not likely] to vary greatly in quantity from day to day.	
10 long are not likely	**11.** Without looking at *Panel A*, see if you can write down three of the items you might find listed on a balance sheet under fixed assets.	

CHECK	FRAME	YOUR ANSWER
11 Land, buildings, plant and machinery, motor vehicles, fixtures and fittings *(any three)*	**12.** Now look at the list of current assets in *Panel A*. Unlike fixed assets, current assets are [intended/not intended] for long-term use in the business.	
12 not intended	**13.** Are the current assets likely to vary in quantity from day to day? _____.	
13 Yes	**14.** Assets intended for comparatively long-term use in the business are called _____ assets.	
14 fixed	**15.** Current assets include cash and assets which will normally be converted into c_____ during the operating cycle of the business.	
15 cash	**16.** In the case of a manufacturing company, the operating cycle is the period between buying the raw materials and selling the finished products. The operating cycle of most businesses is usually less than one year. Current assets, then, include cash and assets which will normally be converted into cash [in the long term/in less than one year].	
16 in less than one year	**17.** Current assets, then, represent employment of money on a short-term basis. Fixed assets, on the other hand, represent the employment of money on a _____-_____ basis.	

CHECK	FRAME	YOUR ANSWER
17 long-term	**18.** On a well-prepared balance sheet, money employed on a long-term or a short-term basis is shown as fixed assets or current assets [together/in separate groups].	
18 in separate groups	**19.** Assets which are likely to be converted into cash during the operating cycle of the business are classed as _____ assets.	
19 current	**20.** Now, the operating cycle of a manufacturing company is the period between buying the _____ _____ and selling the _____ _____.	
20 raw materials finished products	**21.** Stocks of finished products are likely to be sold and therefore to be _____ into _____ during the _____ cycle.	
21 converted cash operating	**22.** Stocks of finished products, raw materials and work in progress are all _____ assets. Such stocks are sometimes referred to as "inventories".	
22 current	**23.** Customers' a_____ are likely to be paid and therefore converted into cash. They are classed as _____ assets.	
23 accounts current	**24.** Marketable securities generally represent short-term investment by the company of its surplus money. They are referred to as "marketable" because they [can/cannot] readily be sold, should the need arise.	

CHECK	FRAME	YOUR ANSWER

24
can

25. Marketable securities are generally classed as _____ assets because they can readily be _____.

25
current
sold

26. Look at the list of assets in *Panel A*. The item below customers' accounts is _____.

26
deposits

Now fold *Panel A* away.
27. When companies make contracts they often have to deposit money as a guarantee that they will fulfil the contracts. These deposits will normally be returned later in cash and are therefore included in the _____ _____.

27
current assets

28. Stocks of raw materials are likely to be processed and sold during the _____ cycle of the business. They are classed as _____ _____.

28
operating
current assets

29. Fixed assets, on the other hand, are not generally acquired with the object of being sold. They are generally acquired for _____-_____ use in the business.

29
long-term

30. Here is a short mixed list of assets: finished products, customers' accounts, land, marketable securities, plant and machinery, cash in banks, raw materials.

Indicate which of the items are current assets and which of them are fixed assets by putting them in two lists under their proper headings. ....

....

CHECK	FRAME	YOUR ANSWER

30

Current: cash in banks, marketable securities, customers' accounts, finished products, raw materials
Fixed: land, plant and machinery

31. Here is a list of assets. One of the items is under the wrong heading. Indicate which one it is.

CURRENT

cash
marketable securities
customers' accounts
raw materials
deposits
prepaid expenses

FIXED

land
buildings
finished products
machinery
motor vehicles
fixtures and fittings

31
finished products

32. Finished products are _____ assets. They are likely to be _____ and therefore converted into cash during the operating cycle of the business.

32
current
sold

LIQUIDITY OF ASSETS
33. In theory all assets could be converted into cash, though normally the _____ assets would not be sold to raise cash.

33
fixed

34. Fixed assets are generally intended for long-term _____ in the _____.

34
use
business

35. An informative balance sheet will list the assets in order of liquidity, i.e. the order in which they could most easily be converted into _____.

CHECK	FRAME	YOUR ANSWER

35
cash

36. Here is the list of assets that you saw before:

CURRENT ASSETS

(1) Cash in banks
   Cash in hand
(2) Marketable securities
   Customers' accounts
   Deposits
   Employee accounts
   Other accounts outstanding
   Prepaid expenses
(3) Finished products
   Work in progress
   Raw materials
   Other supplies

FIXED ASSETS

(4) Land
   Buildings
   Plant and machinery
   Fixtures and fittings
   Motor vehicles

These assets are arranged in four groups, from the most _____ to the least liquid.

36
liquid

37. The fixed assets, then, are the _____ liquid of the assets.

37
least

38. The most liquid single asset of all, of course, is _____ .

38
cash

39. Stocks of finished products, work in progress and raw materials are [more liquid/less liquid] than customers' accounts and marketable securities.

39
less liquid

40. List the following assets in order of liquidity, starting with the most liquid: raw materials, cash in hand, buildings, marketable securities.

CHECK	FRAME	YOUR ANSWER
40 cash in hand (1) marketable securities (2) raw materials (3) buildings (4)	*QUICK ASSETS* **41.** Current assets are more liquid than _____ assets.	
41 fixed	**42.** At the same time some current assets are _____ liquid than other current assets.	
42 more (*or* less)	**43.** In fact some of the current assets are known as quick assets because they can be q_____ converted into cash.	
43 quickly	**44.** Cash, of course, is also a _____ _____.	
44 quick asset	**45.** Customers' accounts can generally be converted into cash at short notice. Customers' accounts are part of the group of current assets which are known as _____ _____.	
45 quick assets	**46.** _____ securities are part of the _____ _____ because they can be sold at short notice.	
46 Marketable quick assets	**47.** The main quick assets, then, are _____, _____ _____ and _____ _____.	
47 cash customers' accounts marketable securities	**48.** Deposits, employee and other accounts, and prepaid expenses are also sometimes included under quick assets because generally they can be .... within a reasonably short period.	

CHECK	FRAME	YOUR ANSWER
48 converted into cash	**49.** Inventories, or stocks, of finished products cannot be sold unless someone is willing to buy them. It [is/is not] always possible to sell them at short notice.	
49 is not	**50.** Inventories of finished products [are/are not] part of the quick assets. Again, inventories of raw materials and work in progress may have to be processed before they can be sold and converted into cash. They [are/are not] quick assets.	
50 are not are not	And that brings us to the end of the third set. Note the time you took to complete the set and the number of frames in which you made a mistake, and enter these details on the Progress Work Sheet. Then read the summary at the beginning of this set once again before going on to the next set.	

2. SET 4. VALUATION OF ASSETS

Estimated time: 25 minutes

Summary

The valuation of assets is always an estimate. The relevant accounting concepts for such estimates of value are described in the "generally accepted accounting standards" of a country. In some countries such standards are required by law.

The general rule is to be cautious. If there is a choice between a higher or lower value of an asset, *almost* always choose the lower value.

Current assets are generally valued at cost or market value, whichever is the lower.

Fixed assets are generally valued at cost or revaluation, less accumulated depreciation.

The figure below shows how each of the assets in *Panel A* is valued.

VALUATION OF ASSETS

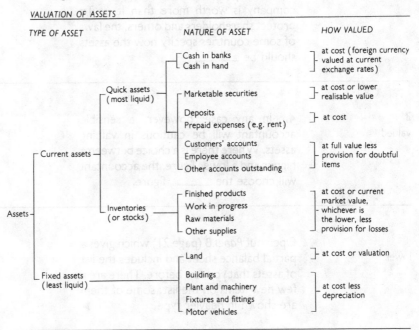

TYPE OF ASSET	NATURE OF ASSET	HOW VALUED
	Cash in banks / Cash in hand	at cost (foreign currency valued at current exchange rates)
Quick assets (most liquid)	Marketable securities	at cost or lower realisable value
	Deposits / Prepaid expenses (e.g. rent)	at cost
Current assets	Customers' accounts / Employee accounts / Other accounts outstanding	at full value less provision for doubtful items
Inventories (or stocks)	Finished products / Work in progress / Raw materials / Other supplies	at cost or current market value, whichever is the lower, less provision for losses
	Land	at cost or valuation
Fixed assets (least liquid)	Buildings / Plant and machinery / Fixtures and fittings / Motor vehicles	at cost less depreciation

CHECK	FRAME	YOUR ANSWER
Is your answer right? Check below.	**1.** In this set we are concerned with the monetary values that are shown on a balance sheet against the different kinds of _____.	
1 assets	**2.** As we pointed out earlier in the introduction, the valuation of assets is not always a simple matter. With some assets, for example, there could be a choice between showing them on the balance sheet at what they cost, and showing them at their current market value. Would cost and current market value always be the same? _____.	
2 No	**3.** If assets are overvalued (shown as too high a value on the balance sheet), this could mislead shareholders and other interested persons into believing that the company is worth more than it is. To protect shareholders and others, the laws of some countries specify how the assets should be _____.	
3 valued	**4.** In any case, however, a sensible accountant will be cautious in valuing assets. Where there is a choice between a higher and a lower figure, the accountant will choose the _____ figure.	
4 lower	Open out *Panel B* (page 21) which gives a partial balance sheet and includes the list of assets that you saw before. There are a few new items on the list; some of them are shown in heavier type. ▶	

CHECK	FRAME	YOUR ANSWER
	5. Look at the figures on the balance sheet in *Panel B*. The total assets are valued at _____ ; the total current assets are shown at _____ ; this includes _____ for cash, _____ for the other quick assets, and _____ for the inventories (or stocks).	
5 356,600 335,400 250 253,850 81,300	**6.** Look at all the entries in heavier type on the balance sheet in *Panel B*. They all [increase/reduce] the value of the assets.	
6 reduce	**7.** Note that the only asset, apart from "goodwill", which is not reduced in some way is the _____ .	
7 cash	*VALUATION OF QUICK ASSETS* **8.** Quick assets, remember, include _____ and other assets that can be _____ converted into cash.	
8 cash quickly	**9.** Quick assets [include/do not include] inventories of finished products and other stocks. They usually [include/do not include] marketable securities, customers' accounts and other accounts.	
9 do not include include	**10.** Look again at *Panel B*. The total of quick assets is _____ + _____ .	

CHECK	FRAME	YOUR ANSWER
10 250 253,850	**11.** Look at the quick assets again. The figure shown against customers' accounts is _____ (how much?). This is the amount actually o_____ to the company by its customers.	
11 261,000 owed	**12.** How much money is owed to the company by its employees? _____.	
12 1,200	**13.** Can the company be certain that it could quickly recover all the money owed to it by customers, employees and other debtors? _____.	
13 No	**14.** It is never certain that all accounts will be fully paid. The company has been cautious and allowed for this fact. One of the entries in heavier type shows that the value of the customers' accounts and other accounts has been [increased/reduced] by _____ (how much?) to allow for accounts that may never be converted into cash.	
14 reduced 11,415	**15.** The total value of the quick assets on the balance sheet is _____.	
15 254,100 (250 + 253,850). *(Note that there are separate totals for cash and for the other quick assets.)*	**16.** Look at the quick assets in *Panel B* once more. The company's marketable securities have been shown at _____ (how much?). This represents their [cost/market value].	

CHECK	FRAME	YOUR ANSWER

16
2,000
cost

17. Marketable securities could be shown at either cost or current market value. However, the market value of these securities can fluctuate widely and so they are usually shown on balance sheets at _____.

17
cost

18. Marketable securities are usually shown at cost, but the balance sheet should indicate their current _____ _____.

18
market value

19. There is one other adjustment that sometimes has to be made to the values given to the quick assets. Normally, quick assets in the form of cash do not have to be adjusted in value. But suppose part of the money is held in foreign currency. In this case the rates of exchange will vary from time to time, and so the v_____ of the c_____ will also vary.

19
value
currency *or* cash

20. Cash assets, then, sometimes have to be adjusted in value when the cash is held in _____ _____.

Incidentally, do you think a fast car is a "quick asset"? _____

20
foreign currency
No!

VALUATION OF INVENTORIES
21. Inventories, or stocks of finished products, partly finished products, raw materials, etc., are part of the _____ assets.

21
current

22. Inventories [are/are not] regarded as part of the quick assets.

CHECK	FRAME	YOUR ANSWER
22 are not	**23.** Until manufactured goods have actually been sold, can a company be quite certain that it will make a profit on them? _____.	
23 No	**24.** A company can never be absolutely certain in advance that it will make a profit on the sale of its goods. It would therefore be unwise to value its inventories at greater than their original cost. Suppose, however, that the market value of the inventories at the date of the balance sheet is less than cost. In this case a cautious management will value its inventories at [cost/market value].	
24 market value	**25.** Thus, inventories of raw materials, finished products, etc., are usually valued at cost or current market value, whichever is the [higher/lower].	
25 lower	**26.** Now look at the lists of these inventories on the balance sheet in *Panel B*. We know that these have been valued at _____ or current _____ value, whichever is the _____.	
26 cost market lower	**27.** In addition, the company has allowed for the fact that some of its stocks may be spoiled (or obsolete). To allow for such stock losses the company has _____ the value of these inventories by 1,100.	
27 reduced	**28.** In other words, the company has apparently been c_____ in valuing its stocks.	

CHECK	FRAME	YOUR ANSWER
28 cautious	*VALUATION OF CURRENT ASSETS* **29.** Let us pause for a moment to summarise what we have been saying in the last two sections, remembering that _____ assets + inventories = current _____ .	
29 quick assets	**30.** One thing we can sometimes see from a balance sheet is whether or not the management has been cautious in _____ the current assets.	
30 valuing	**31.** Customers' accounts and similar accounts usually show the amounts actually _____ to the enterprise. An amount is sometimes [added/subtracted] to allow for estimated non-payment of a certain number of _____ .	
31 owed subtracted accounts	**32.** Quick assets in the form of cash may have to be adjusted in value if the cash is held in a _____ currency.	
32 foreign	**33.** The market value of marketable securities may fluctuate widely. These are therefore usually shown on a balance sheet at _____ .	
33 cost	**34.** At the same time balance sheets should always indicate the _____ _____ of marketable securities.	
34 market value	**35.** Stocks of finished products, raw materials, etc., are usually valued at _____ or current market _____ , whichever	

CHECK	FRAME	YOUR ANSWER

35
cost
value
is the lower

VALUATION OF FIXED ASSETS

36. Fixed assets are valued on a different basis from current assets. Fixed assets, remember, include assets intended for relatively _____-term use in the business.

36
long

37. Most of the fixed assets, such as buildings, plant, machinery and manufacturing tools, will gradually be worn out as they are used. In other words most of the fixed assets will depreciate, or [increase/decrease] in value.

37
decrease

38. Generally, fixed assets are shown on a balance sheet at their original cost with an amount subtracted to allow for the fact that their value has decreased, or depreciated. This allowance is known as d_____.

38
depreciation

39. Look at the balance sheet in *Panel B*. By 31 December 1983 the value of the fixed assets had been reduced by _____ (how much?). In other words 4,600 is the amount of accumulated _____ at 31 December 1983.

39
4,600
depreciation

40. Most of the fixed assets, then, are normally valued at _____ less

_____.

The value shown on the balance sheet for land, however, normally remains at cost. Usually no increase or decrease in the value of the land is recorded on the balance sheet unless the land is actually sold or revalued.

CHECK	FRAME	YOUR ANSWER

40
cost
depreciation

41. To sum up: for the purpose of the balance sheet, land is generally valued at _____. The other fixed assets are valued at ....

41
cost
cost less
depreciation

42. Depreciation reduces the original cost of fixed assets by a certain amount each year over the working life of the asset; that amount is charged as an expense in the profit and loss account. The amount of depreciation charged in any one year will therefore affect the overall profit before income tax; it will thus affect the amount of tax to be paid by a company. The taxation laws of many countries therefore control the rate at which fixed assets can be _____.

42
depreciated

43. The _____ at which fixed assets can be depreciated is often controlled by law. Now look once again at the assets on the balance sheet in *Panel B*. Below the allowance for depreciation there is an entry called _____.

43
rate
goodwill

44. Goodwill is an "intangible" asset and there is nothing concrete to show for it. Goodwill means the advantage, or benefit, that comes from the enterprise's reputation, from its good relations with customers, and so on.

  Because goodwill is intangible it is [easy/difficult] to value.

44
difficult

45. Goodwill is an example of an _____ asset. Such assets are difficult to _____.

CHECK	FRAME	YOUR ANSWER

45
intangible
value

46. Intangible assets are normally included on a balance sheet only when they have been purchased. If an enterprise is bought as a going concern (active business), the price paid may include a certain amount for the goodwill, and this would then be shown on the balance sheet.

Goodwill that has not been bought from someone else will normally [appear/not appear] on the balance sheet.

46
not appear

47. We can assume that the goodwill shown on the balance sheet in *Panel B* has been _____ by our company.

Intangible assets may be shown separately or as part of the _____ assets.

47
bought
fixed

48. When intangible assets are first purchased, they are shown on the balance sheet at cost. When the law permits, like most other fixed assets they are subsequently _____.

48
depreciated

49. To sum up, _____ assets such as goodwill may be shown separately or as part of the [fixed/current] assets. Such assets can be given a money value only when they are _____ from someone else.

49
intangible
fixed
bought

50. When intangible assets are bought, they are normally shown on the balance sheet at _____. Afterwards they may be _____.

But now, is a *really* fast car a quick asset? _____.

CHECK	FRAME	YOUR ANSWER

50	That brings us to the end of Chapter 2.	
cost	Make a note of how long it took you to	
depreciated	complete Set 4 and of the number of	
No!	frames in which you made a mistake, and	
	fill in the Progress Work Sheet. Then	
	reread the summary at the beginning of	
	this set before trying the following	
	questions which will test your knowledge	
	of the two sets in this chapter.	

MINI-TEST ON CHAPTER 2

Now it is time to see how much you have learned. Answer the questions below and, when you have finished, check your answers on the following pages. Then enter the number you answered correctly on the Progress Work Sheet.

1   A balance sheet shows the position of an enterprise [at a particular date/over a period of years].

2   A balance sheet always shows two main groups of figures, the assets and the liabilities. The _____ show what money has been made available to the enterprise from different sources; the _____ show how this money has been employed.

3   In simple words, assets are what is o_____ by an enterprise.

4   _____ assets are acquired for long-term use in the business. Current assets include assets that are likely to be .... during the operating cycle of the business.

5   The operating cycle of most manufacturing companies is usually [more/less] than one year.

6   Fixed assets [are/are not] likely to be converted into cash in the normal course of events.

7   _____ assets represent the enterprise's short-term employment of its funds; _____ assets represent the long-term employment of funds. _____ assets are likely to remain constant in quantity from day to day.

8   Fixed assets often include .... (give three items).

9   Stocks of raw materials, finished products and other supplies are _____ assets.

10   Below is a mixed list of assets. Put a C beside each of the current assets and an F beside each of the fixed assets.

finished products	land	machinery
customers' accounts	cash in banks	buildings
raw materials	marketable securities	

Answers to mini-test on Chapter 2

1 at a particular date.

2 liabilities; assets.

3 owned.

4 Fixed; converted into cash.

5 less.

6 are not.

7 Current; fixed; Fixed.

8 land, buildings, plant and machinery, motor vehicles, *or* fixtures and fittings (*any three*).

9 current.

10 C finished products   F land   F machinery
    C customers' accounts C cash in banks F buildings
    C raw materials   C marketable
                             securities

Mini-test (cont.)

11 Quick assets are part of the _____ assets. They include cash and assets which can normally be ....

12 Inventories, or stocks of raw materials, finished products and other supplies [are/are not] usually regarded as part of the quick assets.

13 A balance sheet will usually show whether or not the management has been _____ in valuing the assets of the company.

14 Stocks of finished goods and other supplies are normally valued at ....

15 Marketable securities are normally shown on a balance sheet at _____, but the balance sheet should always indicate _____ _____.

16 Assets in the form of foreign currency are [never/sometimes] adjusted in value on a balance sheet.

17 Manufacturing tools, plant and buildings are _____ assets. They normally [increase/decrease] in value. Manufacturing tools, plant and buildings are normally valued at ....

18 Land is usually valued at _____.

19 Intangible assets such as goodwill may be shown separately or as part of the _____ assets. Usually they appear on a balance sheet only when they have been _____. When they are first acquired, intangible assets are shown on a balance sheet at _____. Afterwards, they may be _____.

20 The rate at which fixed assets can be depreciated for purposes of taxation is usually controlled by _____.

Answers (cont.)

11 current; quickly converted into cash.

12 are not.

13 cautious.

14 cost or current market value, whichever is the lower.

15 cost; market value.

16 sometimes.

17 fixed; decrease; cost less depreciation.

18 cost.

19 fixed; bought; cost; depreciated.

20 law.

How did you do?

More than 15 correct?	You are doing very well. Go on to Chapter 3.
10-15 correct?	You are making good progress, but read through the summaries of Sets 3 and 4 again, just to consolidate your knowledge before going on to Chapter 3.
Fewer than 10 correct?	It might be a good idea to go back and work through Chapter 2 again.

THE FUNDING SIDE OF THE **3**
BALANCE SHEET – LIABILITIES

3. SET 5. CURRENT LIABILITIES AND FIXED LIABILITIES

Estimated time: 20 minutes

Summary

A company's liabilities are usually listed on a balance sheet in three main groups: current liabilities; fixed liabilities; and shareholders' funds (or owners' equity).

The shareholders are the owners of the company. On the balance sheet the funds they provide are shown separately from those of "outsiders" who have loaned money to the company.

Current and fixed liabilities are together referred to as "outside liabilities".

Fixed liabilities represent the company's long-term finance, and include items on which interest is payable, such as long-term loans from development banks and mortgage loans.

Current liabilities represent the company's short-term finance, and include items like bank short-term loans, bank overdrafts and trade accounts payable.

Interest always has to be paid on bank loans, but most other current liabilities do not require the payment of interest. Apart from bank financing, then, current liabilities generally represent low-cost finance for the company (unless cash discounts are lost). ▶

IMPORTANT NOTE

The balance sheet records *actual* liabilities not financial commitments. Thus, if a company has entered a contract for purchases over ten years this financial fact will *not* appear on the balance sheet. However, the commitment should be revealed in the notes to the financial statements.

CHECK	FRAME	YOUR ANSWER
Is your answer right? Check below.	**I.** A balance sheet is a statement of the assets and _____ of an enterprise at a particular	
1 liabilities point in time (*or* date)	**2.** We have just looked at some typical assets, and in this chapter we shall be dealing with liabilities. In simple terms, the liabilities of an enterprise are what it _____.	
2 owes	**3.** If an enterprise is to function, it must have finance so that it can buy land, buildings and other _____ assets; and so that it can acquire raw materials and other _____ assets.	
3 fixed current	**4.** It is possible to tell how an enterprise has obtained its finance by looking at the _____ on its balance sheet.	
4 liabilities	**5.** On the other hand, the _____ on the balance sheet show how the company has employed this finance.	
5 assets	**6.** Here are the main headings you might find on a balance sheet:	

ASSETS	*LIABILITIES*
Current assets	Current liabilities
Fixed assets	Fixed liabilities
	Shareholders' funds
Total _____	Total _____

Whereas there are two main groups of assets, there are usually _____ main groups of liabilities shown on a balance sheet.

CHECK	FRAME	YOUR ANSWER

6
three

Now open out *Panel C* (page 48) which gives another balance sheet, showing some of the liabilities in more detail.
7. On the balance sheet in *Panel C*, the liabilities are grouped into _____ liabilities, _____ liabilities, and _____ _____.

7
current
fixed
shareholders' funds

8. The shareholders are the owners of the company. The money they have put into the company (the shareholders' funds or owners' equity) is money the company owes to the shareholders. The shareholders' funds are thus part of the total _____ of the company.

8
liabilities

9. The other liabilities of the company are described as "outside" liabilities. These consist of the current _____ and the _____ liabilities.

9
liabilities
fixed

10. The total liabilities of the company thus consist of the shareholders' funds plus the _____ liabilities. The outside liabilities consist of the _____ _____ and the _____ _____.

10
outside
current liabilities
fixed liabilities

OUTSIDE LIABILITIES
11. Now look at the outside liabilities (the current and fixed liabilities) on the balance sheet in *Panel C*. Both groups of liabilities include amounts of money owed to banks and other people. One group does not have to be paid for a relatively long time, while the other group may have to be paid fairly quickly.

Which group of outside liabilities would you say were the long-term liabilities: current liabilities or fixed liabilities?

CHECK	FRAME	YOUR ANSWER
11 fixed liabilities	**12.** Current liabilities usually have to be met, or paid, in the [long/short] term.	
12 short	**13.** _____ liabilities usually have to be met within one year.	
13 Current	**14.** Bank overdrafts are part of the current liabilities. Overdrafts, then, are [short-term/long-term] advances from banks.	
14 short-term	**15.** Accounts with trade creditors (trade accounts payable) and other creditors usually have to be paid [fairly quickly/in the long term]. They are part of the _____ _____.	
15 fairly quickly current liabilities	**16.** Look at the list of current liabilities. It includes bank _____, trade _____ _____, and provision for _____.	
16 overdraft accounts payable taxation	**17.** Bank overdrafts and other current liabilities represent the enterprise's [long-term/short-term] finance.	
17 short-term	**18.** Is it true to say that current liabilities may have to be met within a relatively short period? _____.	
18 Yes	**19.** Current liabilities are usually met from the short-term, or [current/fixed], assets.	
19 current	**20.** This means that an enterprise should generally have enough _____ _____ to cover the current liabilities.	

CHECK	FRAME	YOUR ANSWER
20 current assets	**21.** Look at the first few current liabilities in *Panel C*. Most of them do not involve the payment of interest. Which item in the current liabilities always involves the company in paying interest? _____ _____.	
21 Bank overdraft	**22.** Interest sometimes has to be paid on trade accounts if they are not met within a certain time. However, the only current liability which always involves the payment of interest is _____ _____.	
22 bank overdraft	**23.** Apart from bank overdrafts, then, the current liabilities generally represent [low-cost/expensive] finance for the company.	
23 low-cost	**24.** As a general rule, an enterprise will try to obtain the use of as much _____-cost finance as possible.	
24 low	**25.** Long-term liabilities are known as _____ liabilities.	
25 fixed	**26.** The fixed liabilities represent the company's _____-term finance.	
26 long	**27.** Fixed liabilities may include items like long-term loans from development banks and _____ loans.	
27 mortgage	**28.** To obtain long-term loans, an enterprise usually has to offer some of its property as security. This means that if the enterprise cannot repay the loan when it is due then the _____ may be sold to repay the loan.	

CHECK	FRAME	YOUR ANSWER
28 property	**29.** On the balance sheet in *Panel C* the money raised by mortgage loan amounts to _____. The security for this mortgage is real estate (land and buildings) belonging to the company: in other words, the security is part of the _____ assets.	/
29 8,000 fixed	**30.** Very often companies cannot get long-term loans unless they have _____-term assets to offer as security. Our balance sheet illustrates a special case where a company has a long-term loan from a development bank; this loan is secured on the total _____.	
30 long assets	**31.** Fixed liabilities represent the company's _____-term finance, while current liabilities represent its _____-_____ finance.	
31 long short-term	**32.** Fixed liabilities represent money which has been borrowed for a long period; the company [has to pay/does not have to pay] compensation in the form of interest.	
32 has to pay	**33.** Look at the balance sheet in *Panel C*. The annual interest on the development bank loan is _____ per cent of 50,000 and the annual interest on the mortgage loan is _____ per cent of _____.	
33 10 9 8,000	**34.** The total interest to be paid by the company on its fixed liabilities each year is therefore: _____ + _____ = _____. (The balance sheet shows that 890 of this is still unpaid!)	

CHECK	FRAME	YOUR ANSWER
34 5,000 720 5,720	**35.** In developed countries the interest rates on long-term loans are relatively low. In developing countries, on the other hand, they tend to be _____.	
35 higher	**36.** Where there are not sufficient fixed _____ to offer as security, the interest to be paid on long-term loans, or _____ liabilities, is usually [low/high].	
36 assets fixed high	**37.** What is the total of our company's short-term finance at 31 December 1983? _____.	
37 178,860	**38.** What is the total of the long-term finance at this date? _____	
38 58,000	**39.** Are shareholders' funds (owners' equity) actually repaid to the owners each year? _____.	
39 No	You have now reached the end of Set 5. Once again make a note of the time taken and the number of frames in which you made an error. Then reread the summary at the beginning of this set before going to Set 6. Remember, the glossary is available to help you with any difficult word.	

3. SET 6. SHAREHOLDERS' FUNDS

Estimated time: 15 minutes

Summary

When a company is formed, it needs money to carry on its activities; a good deal of this money usually comes from the shareholders, who buy shares in the company.

The money which the shareholders put into the company in this way is described on the balance sheet as the capital issued.

In return, at the discretion of the directors, the company makes payments to shareholders (pays dividends) out of the profits made by the company.

In addition to the capital issued, shareholders' funds also include capital surplus and earned surplus, which represent profits retained in the business and not paid to shareholders. (Capital surplus and earned surplus will be considered in more detail in the next set.)

CHECK	FRAME	YOUR ANSWER
Is your answer right? Check below.	**1.** In the last set we looked at current and fixed liabilities. The third group making up a company's total liabilities is called _____ _____.	
1 shareholders' funds	*Panel D* gives another form of the balance sheet on *Panel C* which we discussed in the previous set. The balance sheet on *Panel D* shows the shareholders' funds of our company as at 31 December 1983 in more detail. Open out *Panel D* (page 49) before continuing. **2.** The biggest item in the shareholders' funds in December 1983 is the _____ _____.	
2 capital issued	**3.** When a company is formed it needs money so that it can start up its business. A good deal of this money generally comes from the shareholders, who buy _____ in the company.	
3 shares	**4.** The money made available in this way by the shareholders is described on a balance sheet as the capital _____.	
4 issued	**5.** Buying shares in a company involves investing (or lending money) for the life of the _____.	
5 company	**6.** The capital issued can therefore be regarded as [short-term/permanent] finance. We will see later that in return for investing this money the shareholders will expect payments (dividends) from profits made by the company.	

CHECK	FRAME	YOUR ANSWER
6 permanent	**7.** But first look at the other items in the shareholders' funds. As well as the capital issued, the shareholders' funds of our company include capital _____ and _____ surplus.	
7 surplus earned	**8.** In simple terms, capital surplus and earned surplus represent profits that have been retained in the company and not paid to _____.	
8 shareholders	**9.** In other words _____ surplus and _____ surplus are profits that have been _____ in the business.	
9 capital earned retained (*or* kept)	**10.** Earned surplus is profit made in the course of the company's normal operations, whereas _____ _____ is profit that is not made from the normal operations. We will see later in the programme that it may result from the sale of fixed assets, among other things.	
10 capital surplus	**11.** As the shareholders are the owners of the business, any profits retained in the business, together with the capital issued, are in theory owed to the _____.	
11 shareholders	**12.** Capital issued and profits retained in the business therefore appear on our balance sheet as [assets/liabilities] and together they make up the _____ funds.	

CHECK	FRAME	YOUR ANSWER
12 liabilities shareholders'	**13.** Although the shareholders' funds are shown as being owed to the shareholders, they will never be completely paid to the shareholders until the company is wound up. The shareholders' funds can therefore be regarded as p_____ finance.	
13 permanent	**14.** To sum up so far, the company's permanent finance is shown on our balance sheet under the heading _____ _____.	
14 shareholders' funds	**15.** The main items in the shareholders' funds are likely to be _____ _____, _____ _____ and _____ surplus.	
15 capital issued capital surplus earned	*CAPITAL ISSUED AND DIVIDENDS TO SHAREHOLDERS* **16.** We have seen that the capital surplus and earned surplus figures on a balance sheet represent _____ that have been _____ in the company.	
16 profits retained (*or* kept)	**17.** In other words, capital surplus and earned surplus represent profits that [have/have not] been paid to shareholders in the form of dividends.	
17 have not	Before we go on in the next set to consider the difference between capital surplus and earned surplus, let us look briefly at what is meant by shareholders' dividends. **18.** We know that a company always has to pay interest on its fixed liabilities, or _____-term loans.	

CHECK	FRAME	YOUR ANSWER
18 long	**19.** We also know that capital issued represents the money invested by the _____ .	
19 shareholders	**20.** A company does not have to pay interest (as such) on the capital issued, but some compensation will be expected by the _____ .	
20 shareholders	**21.** Where there are sufficient profits the shareholders will naturally expect compensation for the money they have made available to the company, in the form of dividends. The shareholders are compensated by payments known as _____ .	
21 dividends	**22.** Now, all shareholders have rights: for example, the right to share in the _____ made by the company. There may, however, be different classes of shares which carry with them _____ rights.	
22 profits different *(For example, a company may issue preference shares, which give a preferential right to dividends.)*	**23.** However, we are concerned here with the basic class of shares, often known as ordinary shares. Look at the balance sheet in *Panel D*. To find out what shares (or capital) have been issued by the company you have to look at the group of liabilities called [fixed liabilities/shareholders' funds].	
23 shareholders' funds	**24.** Our company, Household Utensils Ltd., has issued 10,000 _____ shares.	

CHECK	FRAME	YOUR ANSWER

24
ordinary

Now fold away *Panel D*.
25. The ordinary shareholders (those who hold ordinary shares) are the basic owners of the company; if the company were to fail, the ordinary shareholders would run the risk of l_____ some or all of their money.

25
losing

26. Note also that the claims of all creditors and other investors have priority over the claims of the ordinary shareholders; if the company failed, the ordinary shareholders' claims on any funds remaining in the company would be the [first/last] to be met.

26
last

27. The ordinary shareholders, then, run [less/more] risk of losing their money than people who give long-term secured loans.

27
more

28. The ordinary shareholders will therefore generally expect to get a [bigger/smaller] return on their money than the interest paid on long-term loans.

28
bigger

29. However, although the ordinary shareholders have a general right to share in the profits of the company, they do not have the right to a fixed _____ each year.

29
dividend (*or* payment)

30. Dividends to shareholders can only be paid out of profits. Thus the amount of any dividend will depend to a certain extent on the size of the _____ made by the _____.

CHECK	FRAME	YOUR ANSWER
30 profits company	**31.** The directors of the company normally recommend each year the amount of _____ that should be paid to the ordinary shareholders.	
31 dividend	**32.** When they are considering what profits are available and how much dividend (if any) should be paid, the directors have to take into account a number of factors. One of these is the needs of the _____ itself.	
32 company	**33.** If there are plans for expanding the company, for example, profits may need to be _____ in the company to finance them.	
33 retained (*or* kept)	**34.** In recommending what amount of dividend is to be paid, the directors also bear in mind the fact that many people prefer to have a fairly steady annual income. The profits made by the company may vary considerably from year to year. Is the dividend paid to the ordinary shareholders likely to vary to the same extent? _____.	
34 No	**35.** Do you think that: (a) shareholders always prefer high dividends? or that (b) shareholders may prefer lower dividends and an increased market value of their shares?	
35 b) (*Remember that shareholders are people; they may want different things at different times.*)	And that brings us to the end of another set. As usual, make a note of the time taken and the number of frames in which you made a mistake. Then reread the summary at the beginning of this set before going on to Set 7.	

3. SET 7. CAPITAL SURPLUS AND EARNED SURPLUS; CAPITAL AUTHORISED AND CAPITAL ISSUED

Estimated time: 15 minutes

Summary

Profits made in the course of the normal operations of an enterprise, and retained in the business, are called earned surplus.

Increased value from the revaluation of fixed assets is called capital surplus.

The amounts on the balance sheet for earned surplus and capital surplus do not reflect the amounts made during the year. Rather, they are the *cumulative totals* for several years up to the date of the balance sheet.

Every properly constituted company is legally able to issue a certain amount of share capital. This is known as its capital authorised.

However, a company may not need all the share capital it is authorised to issue, and the company invites shareholders to contribute only as much money as it actually needs. The amount actually contributed by the shareholders is called the capital issued. It is always either less than or equal to the capital authorised.

IMPORTANT NOTE

The "liability" of a company for shareholders' funds is not a legal liability but it is a useful way to start to learn about balance sheets. In practice, the "liability" is not payable to the owners of a company unless the company is wound up.

Thus, it is more correct to say that the balance sheet shows the assets of a company and how the assets are financed from liabilities and from shareholders' funds.

CHECK	FRAME	YOUR ANSWER
Is your answer right? Check below.	**1.** In the last set we saw that some of the profits made by a company over the years will be paid to shareholders in the form of dividends, and that some will be _____ in the company.	
1 retained (*or* kept)	**2.** Capital surplus and earned surplus represent profits that [have/have not] been paid to shareholders. They are profits held in the business and they form part of the _____ _____.	
2 have not shareholders' funds	**3.** We will see that, if a company makes a profit during any one year, the amount of shareholders' funds is likely to increase. On the other hand, if the company makes a l_____, the amount of these funds will decrease.	
3 loss	**4.** Thus the shareholders' funds shown on the balance sheet are likely to _____ if the company makes a profit during the coming financial year; they will _____ if the company makes a _____.	
4 increase decrease loss	**5.** Now look at the balance sheet in *Panel D* once more. At the end of 1983 how much earned surplus was there? _____.	
5 1,300	**6.** The earned surplus shown on the balance sheet for 31 December 1983 represents: (*a*) profits made during 1983; (*b*) accumulated profits less dividends for several years to 31 December 1983.	

57

CHECK	FRAME	YOUR ANSWER

6
(b) *(The balance sheet is not a statement of results for a particular year: it gives accumulated totals at a particular point in time.)*

7. Earned surplus is part of the profit made by the company as the result of its normal operations. The normal business of our company is manufacturing household goods. Suppose the company revalued some of its land: would this increased value be included in the earned surplus shown on the balance sheet? _____.

7
No *(The company's normal business is manufacturing, not selling land.)*

8. Value arising from the revaluation of fixed assets, then, would generally appear on the balance sheet under the item called _____ _____.

8
capital surplus

9. If during a particular year the company made a loss in the course of its normal operations, then any _____ _____ shown on the balance sheet would be reduced. If the balance sheet showed no earned surplus, then any loss made in the course of normal operations would be deducted from capital surplus.

9
earned surplus

10. In other words, profits made by an enterprise are likely to _____ the shareholders' funds; losses will _____ them.

10
increase
decrease

11. We saw earlier that dividends are paid to shareholders out of profits made by the company; to be more exact, they are paid out of the profits made by the company in the course of its normal operations.
    In other words, dividends are not paid out of _____ surplus.

58

CHECK	FRAME	YOUR ANSWER
11 capital	**12.** The profit, or surplus, made in the course of normal operations in any one year is often known as the company's net profit. Net profit is the p_____ remaining after all expenses have been deducted from income.	
12 profit	**13.** Suppose our company makes a net profit from its normal operations in any one year. Let us see what happens to this. First, all profits are taxed. Some of the net _____, then, will have to be put aside to pay the profits _____.	
13 profit tax	**14.** Of the net profit remaining after tax, some may be paid to shareholders in the form of _____.	
14 dividends	**15.** However, as we have seen, companies normally need to retain some of their profits in the business. There may be future plans requiring finance (or profits may already have been used to finance expansion which has taken place). It is therefore unlikely that all the net profit remaining after allowing for tax will be paid to _____. Some will be _____ in the business.	
15 shareholders retained	**16.** In any year, then, if a company makes a net profit from its normal operations: some will be put aside to pay profits _____; some may be paid to _____ in the form of _____; and some will probably be	

CHECK	FRAME	YOUR ANSWER

16
tax
shareholders
dividends
retained in the
business

17. Net profit, remember, is profit made during the year in the course of the company's _____ _____.

17
normal operations

18. Any net profit that is retained in the business increases the amount of _____ surplus shown on the balance sheet.

18
earned

19. Suppose that the company makes a loss in the course of a year's normal operations. It may still be able to pay dividends out of accumulated _____ _____ from previous years.

19
earned surplus

20. The _____ surplus is always available for paying dividends. Dividends are not paid out of the _____ surplus.

20
earned
capital

HOUSEHOLD UTENSILS LTD.
Balance sheet at 31 December 1983
(expressed in WCU)

ASSETS		LIABILITIES	
Current assets	335 400	Current liabilities	178 860
Fixed assets	21 200	Fixed liabilities	58 000
		Shareholders' funds:	
		Capital authorised *200 000*	
		Capital issued:	
		10 000 ordinary shares	
		of 10 money units each 100 000	
		Capital surplus 8 440	
		Earned surplus 11 300	
		Total shareholders' funds	119 740
Total assets	356 600	Total liabilities	356 600

▶

CHECK	FRAME	YOUR ANSWER

CAPITAL ISSUED AND
CAPITAL AUTHORISED

21. We knew previously how much capital the company had issued: how much had been subscribed by _____.
This amount is _____.

21
shareholders
100 000

22. The balance sheet opposite now shows how much capital the company is legally _____ to issue.

22
authorised

23. Household Utensils Ltd. is legally authorised to issue a total of _____ money units of capital. If the company needs more finance in the future it can therefore invite shareholders to subscribe _____ (how many?) more money units of capital.

23
200,000
100,000 (200,000 minus 100,000)

24. Which of the following is added into the total of the shareholders' funds: [capital authorised/capital issued/ both capital authorised and capital issued]?

24
capital issued

25. The amount of capital that a company is legally permitted to issue is usually known as the _____ _____.

25
capital authorised

26. Companies do not always invite subscription for all the capital which they are legally authorised to issue. One reason is that the company may not be able to employ all this money profitably.
Shareholders, however, will expect compensation for the money which they subscribe, whether it is employed _____ or not.

CHECK	FRAME	YOUR ANSWER
26 profitably	**27.** Thus, it is obviously unwise for a company to have surplus money that cannot be _____ _____.	
27 employed (*or* used) profitably	**28.** In the next chapter we will look at the balance sheet as a whole. But before we finish with the liabilities, there is an important point to note. Suppose our company had made a contract with a supplier which committed it to making certain purchases for the next ten years. Would you learn this from examining the liabilities on the current balance sheet? _____. Would the purchase commitment be revealed in the notes to the financial statements? _____.	
28 No Yes	**29.** Financial obligations of this kind may not appear on the balance sheet but will appear in the .... The balance sheet would include, under liabilities, only the amount due at the _____ of the balance sheet.	
29 notes to the financial statements date	**30.** Balance sheets, then, do not include all of an enterprise's _____ for the future. Incidentally, if you sold that fast car at a profit, would it increase earned surplus or capital surplus? _____ _____.	
30 obligations Earned surplus (*It* *would be part of the* *non-operating* *income for the* *year.*)	You have now reached the end of Chapter 3. Once again make a note on the Progress Work Sheet of the time you took and the number of frames in which you made a mistake before going back to read the summary of Set 7 once more. Then do the mini-test on Chapter 3 to see how much you have remembered.	

MINI-TEST ON CHAPTER 3

Now, see if you can complete this test on the material in Chapter 3. The answers are on the following pages but do not look at them until you have finished the test.

1   It is usually possible to see how an enterprise has obtained its finance by looking at the [assets/liabilities] on its balance sheet.

2   The three main groups of liabilities are usually called _____ _____, _____ _____ and _____ _____.

3   The outside liabilities consist of the ....

4   (a) The _____ _____ represent the permanent finance.
    (b) The _____ _____ represent the short-term finance.
    (c) The _____ _____ represent the long-term finance.

5   Bank overdrafts are [short-term/long-term] advances from banks. They are classed as _____ liabilities.

6   As a rule, an enterprise should be in a position where it can meet its current liabilities from its _____ _____.

7   Capital surplus and _____ surplus are part of the _____ _____.

8   Fixed liabilities are usually _____-term loans.

9   To obtain long-term loans, an enterprise usually has to offer some of its assets as security. As a rule, long-term loans will not be obtainable unless the enterprise has sufficient [current assets/fixed assets] to offer as security.

10 Below is a mixed list of liabilities. Put a C beside the current liabilities, an F beside the fixed liabilities, and an S beside the shareholders' funds.

earned surplus	mortgage loan
bank overdraft	capital issued
trade creditors	capital surplus

Answers to mini-test on Chapter 3

1   liabilities.

2   current liabilities; fixed liabilities; shareholders' funds.

3   current liabilities and the fixed liabilities.

4   (a) shareholders' funds;
    (b) current liabilities;
    (c) fixed liabilities.

5   short-term; current.

6   current assets.

7   earned; shareholders' funds.

8   long.

9   fixed assets.

10 S earned surplus   F mortgage loan
    C bank overdraft   S capital issued
    C trade creditors   S capital surplus

Mini-test (cont.)

11 Interest [has to be paid/does not have to be paid] on bank overdrafts.

12 Where an enterprise does not have sufficient assets to offer as security for long-term loans, the interest charged on these loans is likely to be _____.

13 Apart from bank overdrafts, current liabilities represent [low-cost/expensive] finance for the company.

14 Banks, ordinary shareholders and other creditors all lend money to companies. Which group runs the greatest risk of losing its money?

15 A balance sheet should show not only how much capital has been issued by a company, but also how much capital the company is _____ to issue.

16 Capital surplus represents accumulated profit that [has/has not] been made in the course of an enterprise's normal operations.

17 Is the following statement correct or incorrect? All the net profit made by a company as a result of its normal operations is distributed to the shareholders in the form of dividends. _____.

18 Earned surplus is part of the profit made in the course of _____ _____. Earned surplus represents net profit that has been [distributed to shareholders/retained in the business].

19 If a company makes a loss as a result of its operations in any one year, this will reduce the [current liabilities/fixed liabilities/shareholders' funds] on the balance sheet.

20 When recommending the amount of dividend, the directors must also take into account the financial needs of the _____.

Answers (cont.)

11 has to be paid.

12 high.

13 low-cost.

14 ordinary shareholders.

15 authorised.

16 has not.

17 Incorrect.

18 normal operations; retained in the business.

19 shareholders' funds.

20 company *or* enterprise.

How did you do?

More than 15 correct?	You are doing very well. Go on to Chapter 4.
10-15 correct?	You are making good progress, but why not read through the summaries of Sets 5, 6 and 7 again before going on to Chapter 4?
Fewer than 10 correct?	It might be a good idea to work through this chapter again. Remember to *write down* all your answers!

THE OVERALL
BALANCE SHEET

4

4. SET 8. FINANCIAL STRUCTURE

Estimated time: 30 minutes

Summary

To understand the financial structure of a company, it is important to know the way in which the assets (current and fixed) are financed by the shareholders' funds and the outside liabilities.

By comparing the balance sheet figures for various groups of assets and liabilities we can determine whether or not the company is "solvent" and "liquid".

The enterprise is solvent if assets are greater than outside liabilities. It is liquid if it can meet its current liabilities out of current assets. Current assets less current liabilities is known as net working capital.

Gearing refers to the ratio of shareholders' funds to borrowed money (loan capital). Gearing of 4 : 1 is *low* because four-fifths (80 per cent) of the assets are financed by shareholders' funds and only one-fifth (20 per cent) by borrowed money. By contrast a ratio of 1 : 4 is *high* gearing (high borrowing).

Always *compare* the current balance sheet figures with the previous balance sheet to determine material (significant) changes and ask why such changes have occurred.

Most published balance sheets give two sets of figures (for the current year and for the previous year) to show how the current financial position of the company compares with its previous financial position. A *sources and uses of funds* statement based on such a comparison is also provided. (The sources and uses of funds statement will be discussed in Set 9.)

IMPORTANT NOTE

For the financial management of a business, cash is more important than profit!

CHECK	FRAME	YOUR ANSWER

Is your answer right? Check below.

1. First, open out *Panel E* (page 92). The balance sheet in *Panel E* is dated .... but it also gives the corresponding figures at ....,..........

1
31 December 1984
31 December 1983

2. By examining the balance sheet figures at two dates we can see whether the company's position has _____ between these dates.

2
changed (improved or deteriorated)

THE COMPANY'S POSITION AT THE END OF 1983

3. Before looking at changes, however, let us look at the company's position at the end of 1983, as shown by this balance sheet. The first thing to do is to check that the company is in a position to meet its outside liabilities.

The outside liabilities are the _____ _____ and the _____ _____.

3
current liabilities
fixed liabilities

Now leave *Panel E* for a moment.

SMITH MANUFACTURES LTD.
Balance sheet at 31 December 1983
(expressed in WCU)

ASSETS		LIABILITIES	
Quick assets	180	Current liabilities	180
Inventories	200	Fixed liabilities	200
Land, building, plant, etc.	100	Total outside liabilities	380
		Shareholders' funds	100
Total assets	480	Total liabilities	480

4. So far, we have been looking only at balance sheets which show companies in a position to meet their outside liabilities. But here is another. Can this company meet its outside liabilities out of its total assets? _____.

CHECK	FRAME	YOUR ANSWER

4
Yes

5. Now suppose that shortly after this balance sheet was drawn up the company lost most of its inventories (stocks of finished goods, raw _____, etc.) and its fixed _____ in an earthquake. (The company had not insured against this.) The company would have to reassess its position and might draw up another balance sheet as shown below.

5
materials
assets

SMITH MANUFACTURES LTD.
Balance sheet at 20 January 1984
(expressed in WCU)

	Dec. 1983	Jan. 1984		Dec. 1983	Jan. 1984
ASSETS			LIABILITIES		
Quick assets	180	180	Current liabilities	180	180
Inventories	200	10	Fixed liabilities	200	200
Fixed assets	100	10	Total outside liabilities	380	380
			Shareholders' funds	100	(180)
Total assets	480	200	Total liabilities	480	200

6. In January 1984 the value of the assets has been greatly reduced, but the outside liabilities still remain. The balance sheet still balances (because the shareholders' funds now show a negative amount); let us see whether the company can still meet its outside liabilities out of its total assets.

The total assets in January 1984 are _____ (figures). The outside liabilities at that date are _____ (figures).

6
200
380

7. The company, then, cannot meet its _____ _____ out of its _____ _____.

CHECK	FRAME	YOUR ANSWER
7 outside liabilities total assets	**8.** In this example the balance sheet shows that the company was not solvent in January 1984. A company is said to be solvent if it can meet its _____ _____ out of its _____ _____.	
8 outside liabilities total assets	Now let us return to *Panel E* (page 92) and check to make sure that the company shown there was solvent at the end of 1983. **9.** At 31 December 1983 the total assets were _____ (figures) and the outside liabilities were _____ (figures).	
9 356,600 236,860	**10.** At the end of 1983, then, our company was _____.	
10 solvent	**11.** An enterprise is said to be solvent if its _____ _____ are greater than its _____ _____.	
11 total assets outside liabilities	**12.** Now, an enterprise will not have to meet all its outside liabilities in the short term: in other words, it will not have to meet both the current and fixed liabilities in the short term. However, it may have to meet the _____ liabilities in the short term.	
12 current	**13.** Any enterprise should therefore have enough [current assets/fixed assets] to cover its current liabilities.	
13 current assets (*Fixed assets are not converted into cash, as a rule.*)	**14.** An enterprise is said to be liquid if it can meet its _____ liabilities out of its current assets.	

CHECK	FRAME	YOUR ANSWER
14 current	**15.** Remember that an enterprise is _____ if it can meet its outside liabilities out of its total assets; it is _____ if it can meet its current liabilities out of its current assets.	
15 solvent liquid	**16.** Now see whether our company was liquid at the end of 1983. To do this we must look at the _____ _____ and the _____ _____.	
16 current liabilities current assets	**17.** The total current liabilities at 31 December 1983 were _____ and the total current assets were _____.	
17 178,860 335,400	**18.** In other words, the current liabilities [were/were not] covered by the current assets. Therefore, the company was _____ at the end of 1983.	
18 were liquid	**19.** Now, working capital equals current assets minus current liabilities. At 31 December 1983 our company had working capital of 335,400 (current assets) − _____ (current liabilities) = _____.	
19 178,860 156,540	**20.** The greater the excess of current assets over current liabilities, the [less/more] working capital the company has.	
20 more	**21.** In other words, a company has working capital as long as it is liquid. If a company is not liquid it has no _____ _____.	

CHECK	FRAME	YOUR ANSWER
21 working capital	**GEARING** **22.** Now let us compare the share-holders' funds at the end of 1983 with the total finance employed by the company. You can find the total finance employed by an enterprise by looking at the figure for the total assets or for the total liabilities. Both these figures are the _____ since both sides of the _____ sheet always balance.	
22 same balance	**23.** Shareholders' funds at the end of 1983 were _____ and the total finance employed by the company at that date was _____.	
23 119,740 356,600	**24.** Let us find what proportion of the total finance employed by the company the shareholders' funds represented. Since: $$\frac{119{,}740 \times 100}{356{,}600} = \text{approx. 33 per cent,}$$ at the end of 1983 the shareholders' funds represented approximately one-third of the total _____ employed by the company.	
24 finance	**25.** As we discussed in Chapter 3, all a company's funds are borrowed either from the shareholders (who _____ the company), or from persons outside the company (the outside _____).	
25 own liabilities	**26.** In our present example, the difference between the total finance and the shareholders' funds (356,600 − 119,740 = _____) represents the outside liabilities (money borrowed from sources other than the _____).	

CHECK	FRAME	YOUR ANSWER
26 236,860 shareholders	**27.** Now, the ratio of shareholders' funds to borrowed money is known as the gearing of a company. G_____ refers to the ratio of shareholders' funds to borrowed money.	
27 Gearing	**28.** Thus in our present example, the ratio of 119,740 : 236,860 is the ratio of shareholders' funds to borrowed money. This ratio reflects the _____ of the company.	
28 gearing	**29.** Rounding these numbers up to the nearest 10,000, we have the ratio of 120,000 : 240,000, or 1 : 2. The figures on the balance sheet at *Panel E* thus represent a g_____ of _____.	
29 gearing 1 : 2	**30.** Note that the gearing is sometimes calculated as the ratio of shareholders' funds to long-term loan capital only (the fixed liabilities). In our calculations in frames 26 to 29 above, the figure for borrowed money includes both the short-term loans (current _____) and the long-term loans (_____ liabilities).	
30 liabilities fixed	*CHANGES BETWEEN 1983 AND 1984* **31.** Now let us see what changes have taken place between the end of 1983 and the end of 1984. First look at the total finance at the two dates. In 1983 this was _____ and in 1984 it is _____.	
31 356,600 286,980	**32.** In other words, the company had [more/less] total finance in 1984.	

CHECK	FRAME	YOUR ANSWER

32 less	**33.** The total liabilities have decreased by December 1984, and this decrease is accompanied by a corresponding decrease in the total _____.	
33 assets	**34.** We can see how this overall change has come about. Look at the three main groups of liabilities at the two dates. Which group shows the biggest change between December 1983 and December 1984? _____ _____.	
34 Current liabilities	**35.** The total current liabilities have [increased/decreased] from _____ to _____ (figures).	
35 decreased 178,860 82,974	**36.** Now, the current liabilities show a particularly big change in one item; the _____ _____ has been [increased/reduced] from _____ to _____.	
36 bank overdraft reduced 84,160 10,520	**37.** This means that the company has to pay less _____ on its bank overdraft.	
37 interest	**38.** Now, if the current liabilities show a big decrease we might expect to find a big decrease also in the current _____.	
38 assets (*Current liabilities are usually met from current assets.*)	**39.** Let us look at the current assets at the two dates. The total has [increased/decreased] from _____ (figure) in 1983 to _____ (figure) in 1984.	

74

CHECK	FRAME	YOUR ANSWER

39
decreased
335,400
267,000

40. This suggests that the company has used some of its _____ _____ to pay off the _____ liabilities.

40
current assets
current

41. The biggest single change in the current assets is that the _____ _____ have been reduced from _____ (figure) to _____ (figure).

41
customers' accounts
261,000
180,000

42. The company also sold its _____ _____ in 1984.

42
marketable
securities

43. The current liabilities, then, show a big change between the two dates.
    Look at the other two groups of liabilities. Have the fixed liabilities changed? _____.

43
No

44. Look at the shareholders' funds. Between December 1983 and December 1984 the total has [decreased/increased] from _____ to _____.

44
increased
119,740
146,006

45. In other words, the shareholders' holding in the company has increased. We can see what has caused this change in the shareholders' funds.
    For one thing, the company has issued additional _____ to the value of _____.
    Secondly, the earned surplus has increased from _____ to _____.

CHECK	FRAME	YOUR ANSWER

45
capital
20,000
11,300
17,566

46. To sum up the main changes on the balance sheet between 31 December 1983 and 31 December 1984: the total liabilities [increased/decreased] from _____ to _____ ; the current liabilities [increased/decreased] and in particular the _____ _____ was reduced; the current assets [increased/decreased]; the main change here was in the _____ _____ ; and also the shareholders' funds [increased/decreased]; the main reason for this was that more ....
....

46
decreased
356,600
286,980
decreased
bank overdraft
decreased
customers' accounts
increased
capital was issued

47. As the total liabilities have decreased, this means that the company is employing less total _____ at the end of 1984.

47
finance (*or* money)

48. We can see whether the proportion of shareholders' funds in the total finance has also changed.

In December 1984 the company's total finance is 286,980. At this date the shareholders' funds amount to _____ .

48
146,006

49. In other words, in 1984 the shareholders' funds represent:

$$\frac{146,006 \times 100}{286,980} = \text{approx. 50 per cent}$$

of the _____ _____ .

CHECK	FRAME	YOUR ANSWER
49 total finance	**50.** Now look back to frame 24: at the end of 1983 the shareholders' funds represented 33 per cent of the total _____ .	
50 finance	**51.** The proportion of shareholders' money in the company at the end of 1984, then, is [greater/smaller] than at the end of 1983.	
51 greater	**52.** Let us look at this change in terms of changes in the gearing of the company. Gearing is the ratio of _____ _____ to borrowed money.	
52 shareholders' funds	**53.** At the end of 1984 borrowed money (total finance − shareholders' funds) = 286,980 − _____ = _____ .	
53 146,006 140,974	**54.** At the end of 1984, therefore, it is evident that the gearing of the company is 146,006 : _____ , which is very nearly 1 : 1.	
54 140,974	**55.** From the end of 1983 to the end of 1984 the gearing has gone down from 1 : 2 to _____ .	
55 1 : 1	**56.** The higher the proportion of borrowed money to shareholders' funds, the higher the gearing. If the gearing is 1 : 4, four-fifths (or _____ per cent) of the total finance comes from borrowed money. This is a high proportion so we say the _____ is high.	

77

CHECK	FRAME	YOUR ANSWER

56
80
gearing

57. If the gearing is 4 : 1, only _____ - _____ (or 20 per cent) of the total finance comes from _____ _____. This is a low proportion, so we say the gearing is _____.

Gearing of about 2 : 1, in which _____ - _____ (that is, approximately 33 per cent) of the total finance comes from borrowed money is considered normal.

57
one-fifth
borrowed money
low
one-third

THE COMPANY'S POSITION AT THE END OF 1984

58. Now that we have looked at the main changes between the two dates, just check the company's general position at the end of 1984.

We find that the total assets at 31 December 1984 are _____ (figures). The total outside liabilities are : _____ + _____ = _____. Therefore, the company is _____.

58
286,980
82,974
58,000
140,974
solvent

59. An enterprise is said to be solvent when its _____ _____ are covered by its _____ _____.

59
outside liabilities
total assets

60. Now see whether the company is still liquid at the end of 1984. An enterprise is said to be liquid when its _____ _____ are covered by ....

60
current liabilities
its current assets

61. In December 1984 our company's current liabilities are valued at _____ and the current assets at _____.

CHECK	FRAME	YOUR ANSWER

| 61
 82,974
 267,000 | **62.** This means that the company is able to meet its _____ _____ out of its _____ _____. In other words, the company is _____ at the end of 1984. | |

| 62 <br> current liabilities <br> current assets <br> liquid | **63.** Can the company also meet its current liabilities out of its quick assets in December 1984? At that date the quick assets are valued at:
 _____ + _____ = _____. | |

| 63
 450
 179,550
 180,000 | **64.** In other words, at 31 December 1984 the company could, if necessary, meet its _____ _____ out of its _____ _____. | |

| 64 <br> current liabilities <br> quick assets | In this set we introduced the idea of looking at changes in a company's financial position from one balance sheet to the next. We take this idea further in the next set as we look at the sources and uses of funds statement. Before going on to that, however, note the time you took to complete this set and the number of frames in which you made a mistake before reading through the summary for this set once again. | |

4. SET 9. SOURCES AND USES OF FUNDS

Estimated time: 20 minutes

Summary

The sources and uses of funds statement is developed by comparing the current balance sheet with that of the previous period and using some other data.

The sources and uses of funds statement shows the changes that have taken place in the period between the two balance sheets in terms of *new funds* available to the business and how they have been used; it shows where new money has come from (sources) and how it has been used (uses).

Sources of new funds may be any of the following:
- net profit (after depreciation);
- depreciation;
- new share capital issued;
- sale of fixed assets;
- new loans.

Depreciation is not exactly a source of new funds but it reduces the net profit for the period. Since no money for depreciation actually leaves the business, the source of funds is net profit before depreciation, which is the same as net profit after depreciation, plus depreciation.

The uses of funds may be any of the following:
- payment of dividends;
- purchase of fixed assets;
- repayment of loans or capital;
- increase in net working capital.

Sources of funds always equal uses. Any funds not used for the special purposes above result in changes in net working capital (current assets less current liabilities). ▶

IMPORTANT NOTE

The sources and uses of funds statement reveals the key financial management decisions for the accounting period.

CHECK	FRAME	YOUR ANSWER
Is your answer right? Check below.	**1.** The total finance available to a company usually does not remain the same from year to year. Common sense might suggest that the more a company's total _____ increases from year to year, the better the company is doing.	
1 finance	**2.** However, it is not quite as simple as that. A company whose total finance has increased from one year to the next may not be in as healthy a position as one whose _____ _____ has not increased. It all depends on where the money has come from and what it has been spent on.	
2 total finance	**3.** For example, a company whose total finances increased by 10,000 world currency units (WCU) as a result of an [increase/decrease] in earned surplus (or "profits") is probably in a healthier financial position than one which had no increase in earned surplus but which showed an increase of 20,000 WCU in its total finance as a result of the issue of new share c_____.	
3 increase capital	**4.** But again an increase in share capital may or may not be a sign of financial health. It all depends on what the money is _____ on.	
4 spent	**5.** On the one hand, the money may be spent on modernising plant and equipment so that a substantial _____ in profits may be expected in the future.	

CHECK	FRAME	YOUR ANSWER
5 increase	**6.** On the other hand, the money might be spent on the purchase of property for the use of directors or top management, which is less likely to lead to an increase in _____ for the company.	
6 profits	**7.** In other words, when new money comes into a business, it is important in assessing the company's financial position to know where the money has come from and what it has been _____ on.	
7 spent	**8.** The sources and uses of funds statement (sometimes called the funds flow statement) is a document which is often attached to the balance sheet, and gives information about the sources and _____ of new money which has come into the company since the time of the previous _____ sheet.	
8 uses balance	**9.** In other words, the _____ and uses of funds statement is concerned with ch_____ that have taken place in a company's finances between one balance sheet and the next.	
9 sources changes	**10.** The sources and uses of funds statement is itself a sort of balance sheet. On the one side is a summary of where various amounts of money have come from, and on the other, a summary of what various amounts of money have been spent on. The total of the sums of money on the "sources" side must e_____ the total of the sums of money on the "_____" side.	

CHECK	FRAME	YOUR ANSWER
10 equal uses	**11.** The _____ and _____ of funds statement will show the changes that have taken place in a company's finances in respect of: share capital, long-term loans, fixed assets and depreciation, net profit and dividends, and working capital.	
11 sources uses	**12.** If new share capital has been issued this will be reflected as a [source/use] of funds.	
12 source	**13.** On the other hand, if money has been returned to shareholders (in other words, if some of the capital has been repaid), this will be listed under the _____ of funds.	
13 uses	**14.** Similarly, if new long-term loans have been taken out, this is a _____ of funds, whereas if long-term loans have been repaid, this will be reflected under the .... (Note that as short-term loans are part of the current liabilities, they are accounted for in the calculation of working capital. This will be discussed later in the set.)	
14 source uses of funds	**15.** Look at the balance sheet on *Panel E* once again and answer the following questions about changes in the finances of Household Utensils Ltd. between 31 December 1983 and 31 December 1984. Share capital has increased by 20,000 units. On a sources and uses of funds statement this would be listed as a _____ of funds. Have any long-term loans been repaid, or new ones raised? _____.	

CHECK	FRAME	YOUR ANSWER
15 source No	**16.** The purchase of fixed assets during a financial year will increase the value of the _____ assets shown on the balance sheet and the sale of fixed assets will d_____ this value.	
16 fixed decrease	**17.** If the valuation of fixed assets on the balance sheet goes down from one year to the next, this means that more money has come in from the _____ of fixed assets than was spent on the purchase of new ones. This inflow of money is new money coming into the company, so any decrease in the valuation of fixed assets will be reflected as a _____ of funds on the sources and uses of funds statement.	
17 sale source	**18.** Conversely, any increase in the valuation of the fixed assets will indicate the outflow of money for the purchase of fixed assets, and will therefore be reflected on a sources and uses of funds statement under the _____ of _____ .	
18 uses funds	**19.** The figures we enter on the sources and uses of funds statement are calculated from the valuation of the fixed assets before depreciation has been deducted. Looking again at *Panel E*, we see that the valuation of the fixed assets (before depreciation has been deducted) has increased from 24,800 in 1983 to 26,200 in 1984. In other words, funds have been used to purchase fixed assets during the year. Therefore, the figure we should enter under the uses of funds is 26,200 − 24,800 = _____ .	

CHECK	FRAME	YOUR ANSWER
19 1,400 *(the increase in the* *valuation* *of fixed assets* *before depreciation)*	**20.** Although depreciation is a sum of money deducted from the valuation of _____ _____ on the balance sheet, this money is not actually spent but is retained by the company.	
20 fixed assets	**21.** Depreciation is a provision made on the balance sheet for the expenses which will be involved when _____ equipment has to be bought to replace old equipment. The money however [does/does not] leave the business until the new assets are actually bought.	
21 new does not	**22.** Until the new fixed assets are bought, then, the company has the funds identified as depreciation available to it. The figure for depreciation therefore reflects a [source/use] of funds.	
22 source	**23.** Returning to *Panel E* once more we see that in preparing a sources and uses of funds statement for this balance sheet we would enter a sum of _____ (7,220 – 4,600) in respect of depreciation under the sources of funds; and at the same time we would enter a sum of 1,400 in respect of the purchase of fixed assets under the _____ of funds.	
23 2,620 uses	**24.** Note that we would enter 2,620 for depreciation, and not 7,220 since in the sources and uses of funds statement we are concerned only with the _____ occurring between one balance sheet and the next.	

CHECK	FRAME	YOUR ANSWER

24
changes

25. The figure on the balance sheet for earned surplus reflects the accumulated profits of a company after dividends have been paid. Any increase in the earned surplus from one year to the next thus reflects profits retained in the business and this is clearly a [source/use] of funds for the enterprise.

25
source

26. On the balance sheet on *Panel E*, we can see that the increase in earned surplus between 1983 and 1984 was _____ (17,566 – 11,300) units.

26
6,266

27. This _____ of funds, together with that part of the profit that was set aside for the payment of dividends, would be reflected in the sources and uses of funds statement under "net profit for the period". In this case, the sum set aside for dividends was 5,000 units. So the net profit was 11,266 (6,266 + _____) units. (In Set 12 on the profit and loss account you will see how the figure for net profit is worked out.)

27
source
5,000

28. It is at the discretion of a company's directors whether profits are retained in the business or paid out to shareholders in the form of _____. Money paid out as dividends represents an outflow of money and would be reflected on a sources and uses of funds statement as one of the _____ of _____.

28
dividends
uses
funds

29. And finally we come to the most difficult part: working capital. You may remember that in Set 8 we defined working capital as equal to current _____ minus _____ liabilities.

CHECK	FRAME	YOUR ANSWER

29
assets
current

30. Working capital equals current assets minus current liabilities. We can see from this formula that if current assets increase and current liabilities do not (or at least if current liabilities increase by less than the _____ _____ have done), then working capital will increase.

30
current assets

31. What sort of situation results in an increase in current assets?

One example would be increased inventory; another example would be increased receivables. In either case money is not coming in, but rather is being used for some purpose.

Now as we saw in the previous frame, an increase in current assets (when money is being _____) will usually result in an increase in _____ _____.

31
used
working capital

32. We can thus see that an increase in working capital would be entered on the sources and uses of funds statement as a _____ of funds.

32
use

33. To make these relationships more clear, let us go back to frame 30 and the formula: working capital equals current assets minus current _____.

We saw there that if current assets increase, _____ capital will tend to increase.

33
liabilities
working

34. Now if current assets decrease, working _____ will also decrease (unless current liabilities go down by an even greater amount).

CHECK	FRAME	YOUR ANSWER
34 capital	**35.** Current assets decrease when, for example, inventories and receivables become lower. However, if one current asset changes for another (e.g. accounts receivable are settled in cash), this does not change the total current assets. Thus, only a decrease in total current _____ causes an inflow of funds.	
35 assets	**36.** As we saw in frame 34, when current assets decrease, working capital will also tend to _____. So a decrease in working capital means an inflow of funds, and any decrease in working capital would be entered on the sources and uses of funds statement as a _____ of funds.	
36 decrease source	**37.** In preparing a sources and uses of funds statement we need to calculate how the amount of working capital has _____ from one balance sheet to the next.	
37 changed	**38.** Let us do this for the balance sheet figures shown on *Panel E.* As at 31 December 1983, working capital = 335,400 − _____ = _____.	
38 178,860 156,540	**39.** As at 31 December 1984, working capital = _____ − 82,974 = _____.	
39 267,000 184,026	**40.** So, from 31 December 1983 to 31 December 1984, working capital [increased/decreased] by 184,026 − 156,540 = _____.	

CHECK	FRAME	YOUR ANSWER

40
increased
27,486

41. On a sources and uses of funds statement we would therefore reflect an increase in working capital of 27,486 as one of the [sources/uses] of funds.

41
uses

42. Finally, let us put all this together in a concise statement. Look at the following sources and uses of funds statement and fill in the missing words or figures where indicated by referring back to the calculations we have carried out in the earlier frames of this set.

HOUSEHOLD UTENSILS LTD.
*Sources and uses of funds statement
for the year to 31 December 1984
(expressed in WCU)*

SOURCES OF FUNDS

Net profit for the period (after depreciation charged)	11 266
..........................(a) (added back)	2 620
New share capital issued	(b) ....
Total sources of new funds	33 886

USES OF FUNDS

Dividends paid	5 000
Purchase of fixed assets	1 400
.................(c) in net working capital	(d) ....
Total uses of new funds	33 886

NET WORKING CAPITAL COMPUTATION

	1983	1984
Current assets	335 400	267 000
Current liabilities	178 860	82 974
	156 540	184 026
Increase in net working capital		27 486

CHECK	FRAME	YOUR ANSWER

CHECK	FRAME	YOUR ANSWER
42 (a) Depreciation (b) 20,000 (c) Increase (d) 27,486	**43.** The sources of funds were: Net profit .... Depreciation .... New capital .... Total 33 886	
43 11,266 2,620 20,000	**44.** The uses of funds were: Dividends .... Fixed assets purchased .... Increase in net working capital .... Total 33 886	
44 5,000 1,400 27,486	**45.** Thus, the sources and uses of funds statement reveals the key _____ management decisions during the period.	
45 financial	You have now reached the end of the most difficult set in the book. Perhaps you should take a good break. Before trying the next chapter, enter the usual data on the Progress Work Sheet, read the summary for this set again and then tackle the mini-test on Chapter 4.	

MINI-TEST ON CHAPTER 4

Now test yourself again. Check your answers and enter your results on the Progress Work Sheet.

1   An enterprise is said to be *solvent* if it can meet its _____ _____ out of its _____ _____ .

2   An enterprise is said to be *liquid* if it can meet its _____ _____ out of its _____ _____ .

3   Current assets − _____ _____ = working capital.

4   If a company has a gearing of 1 : 3, _____ per cent of its cost of assets is financed by shareholders' funds. This gearing is [high/low].

Open out *Panel X* opposite.

---

5   This gives the balance sheet of _____ _____ Ltd. at ....

6   This balance sheet also gives the figures at ....

7   Look at the company's position in December 1983. Was the company solvent in December 1983? _____ . Why? ....

8   Was the company liquid in December 1983? _____ . Why? ....

9   Is the company solvent in December 1984? _____ .

10 Is the company liquid in December 1984? _____ .

11 Between December 1983 and December 1984 the total finance employed by the company [increased/decreased] from _____ to _____ .

12 The biggest change was in the [current liabilities/fixed liabilities/shareholders' funds], which [increased/decreased] from _____ to _____ .

Answers to mini-test on Chapter 4

1 outside liabilities; total assets.

2 current liabilities; current assets.

3 current liabilities.

4 25; high.

5 Steel Products; 31 December 1984.

6 31 December 1983.

7 Yes. Because the total assets were greater than the outside liabilities.

8 Yes. Because the current assets were greater than the current liabilities.

9 Yes.

10 Yes.

11 decreased; 54,534; 50,629.

12 fixed liabilities; decreased; 13,000; 8,500.

Mini-test (cont.)

13 The main group of assets showing the biggest change was the _____ assets; which [increased/decreased] from _____ to _____.

14 Fill in the missing figures in the following table of liabilities for Steel Products Ltd.:

December 1983		%	*December 1984*		%
Current	....	29	Current	....	29
Fixed	....	24	Fixed	....	17
Shareholders' funds	....	47	Shareholders' funds	....	54
Total	54 534	100	Total	50 629	100

15 In which year were the shareholders' funds a higher proportion of the total finance: 1983 or 1984? _____.

16 The sources and uses of funds statement gives details of where _____ money acquired by an enterprise comes from, and what it has been spent on.

17 Reduction of working capital is regarded as a _____ of funds.

18 Which of the following is not a source of funds: new capital issued, sale of fixed assets, increase in working capital and depreciation?

19 Any dividends paid by a company are a _____ of funds.

20 A company whose total finance has increased from one balance sheet to the next is always in a better financial position than one whose total finance has not increased. True or false? _____.

Answers (cont.)

13 fixed; decreased; 30,925; 26,902.

14	15,974	14,874
	13,000	8,500
	25,560	27,255

15 1984.

16 new.

17 source.

18 increase in working capital.

19 use.

20 False.

How were your results?

More than 15 correct?	Well done! Go straight on to Chapter 5.
10-15 correct?	Reasonably good. Run over the summaries of Sets 8 and 9 before going further, however.
Fewer than 10 correct?	This was a difficult chapter. Give yourself a break and then try the chapter again. It will seem much easier next time.

MEASURING SOLVENCY AND LIQUIDITY 5

5. SET 10. SOLVENCY

Estimated time: 25 minutes

Summary

Solvency is measured by the solvency ratio expressed as a percentage. The solvency ratio indicates the proportion of shareholders' funds in the total liabilities. The higher the solvency ratio, the higher the proportion of shareholders' funds in the total financing of the business.

When the business expands, the solvency ratio may either increase or decrease depending upon the source of funds to finance the expansion. Similarly, it may increase or decrease when the company contracts.

It is the gearing of the company which shows how assets are financed by shareholders' funds (owners' equity) or outside liabilities.

A *high* solvency ratio (high shareholders' funds) represents *low* gearing, *low* risk and good potential for borrowing more outside finance (higher debt capacity).

A *low* solvency ratio (low shareholders' funds) indicates *high* gearing, *high* risk and less potential for borrowing more outside finance (lower debt capacity).

CHECK	FRAME	YOUR ANSWER
Is your answer right? Check below.	**1.** An enterprise is said to be solvent if its total assets are greater than its outside _____. So the solvency of an enterprise is its ability to meet its _____ liabilities.	
1 liabilities outside	**2.** Now, a company can be solvent to a greater or lesser degree. The more the _____ _____ relatively exceed the _____ _____, the greater is the degree of solvency.	
2 total assets outside liabilities		

ASSETS	%	LIABILITIES	%
Current assets	52	Current liabilities	26
Fixed assets	48	Fixed liabilities	19
			45
		Shareholders' funds	55
Total assets	100	Total liabilities	100

3. If we want to compare an enterprise's degree of solvency at two dates, it is helpful to use ratios or percentages. Look at the above table of assets and liabilities; they are expressed here as percentages.

The "solvency ratio" is a useful measure of solvency and it is very often expressed as a percentage. The percentage used is the difference between the total assets and the outside liabilities.

From the above table we can work out that the solvency ratio is _____ per cent less _____ per cent = _____ per cent.

CHECK	FRAME	YOUR ANSWER
3 100, 45, 55	**4.** Look at the table again: 55 per cent is the proportion of _____ _____ in the total liabilities.	
4 shareholders' funds	**5.** In other words, the _____ _____ indicates the proportion of shareholders' funds in the _____ _____.	
5 solvency ratio total liabilities (*or* total finance)	**6.** The higher the solvency ratio, the [higher/lower] is the proportion of _____ _____ in the total liabilities.	
6 higher shareholders' funds	**7.** Remember that the solvency ratio also indicates how easily the enterprise can meet its _____ liabilities out of its _____ _____.	
7 outside total assets	**8.** Therefore the greater the proportion of shareholders' funds in the total finance employed by the company, the more easily can the company meet its _____ liabilities.	
8 outside	Let us now return to *Panel E*. **9.** Now, in December 1983 the shareholders' funds were _____ per cent of the total finance. (Look at Set 8, frame 24, if you cannot remember.)	
9 33	**10.** Therefore the _____ ratio in December 1983 was _____ per cent.	
10 solvency 33	**11.** In December 1984, on the other hand, the shareholders' funds were _____ per cent of the total finance. (Look at Set 8, frame 49, if necessary.) Therefore the _____ _____ was _____ per cent.	

CHECK	FRAME	YOUR ANSWER

11 50 solvency ratio 50	**12.** In 1984, then, the company had a greater excess of _____ _____ over _____ _____ than in 1983.	
12 total assets outside liabilities	**13.** In other words, in 1984, the shareholders' funds were a _____ proportion of the _____ _____ than in 1983.	
13 greater total liabilities (*or* total finance)		

COMPANY A

31 December 1982

ASSETS	%	LIABILITIES	%
Current assets	40	Current liabilities	25
Fixed assets	60	Fixed liabilities	25
		Shareholders' funds	50
Total assets	100	Total liabilities	100

14. Changes in the solvency ratio are important, but as they can occur for a number of reasons, we cannot draw simple conclusions from such changes. As we shall see, an increase in the solvency ratio can be a sign either that the enterprise is expanding or that it is contracting. Similarly, we shall see that a decrease in the solvency ratio can be the result of either expansion or contraction.

Look at the above table of assets and liabilities given in percentages.

At 31 December 1982 we see that the solvency ratio of Company A was _____ per cent.

CHECK	FRAME	YOUR ANSWER

14
50

15. Now Company A was a successful and profitable enterprise. In 1983 the directors planned an expansion of its trading activities and they retained a substantial amount of the 1983 trading profits in the business to finance this _____.

15
expansion

COMPANY A
LIABILITIES

	31 Dec. 1982 Units	%	31 Dec. 1983 Units	%
Current liabilities		4 000	25		5 000	25
Fixed liabilities		4 000	25		4 000	20
Shareholders' funds:					
Capital issued	5 000			5 000	
Capital surplus	1 000			1 000	
Earned surplus	2 000			5 000	
		8 000	50		11 000	55
Total		16 000	100		20 000	100

16. The table above shows the liabilities (in units and in percentages) of Company A in both December 1982 and December 1983.

In December 1982 the solvency ratio was _____ per cent and in December 1983 it was _____ per cent.

16
50
55

17. We can see what has caused this change in the solvency ratio. First, the total finance has [increased/decreased]. The current liabilities have increased to some extent but the biggest single change in the liabilities is that the _____ _____ has increased from 2,000 to 5,000.

CHECK	FRAME	YOUR ANSWER

17
increased
earned surplus

18. Those profits arising from normal operations and retained in the business appear on the balance sheet under _____ surplus.

18
earned

19. In this case, then, the main reason for the increase in the solvency ratio is that the _____ _____ has increased.

19
earned surplus

20. The earned surplus increased because more _____ were retained in the business to finance the _____ of the company's activities.

20
profits
expansion

21. In other words, the solvency ratio increased in this particular case because the company was _____.

21
expanding

COMPANY A
LIABILITIES

	Dec. 1982 Units	%	Dec. 1983 Units	%	Dec. 1984 Units	%
Current liabilities	4 000	25	5 000	25	5 000	22
Fixed liabilities	4 000	25	4 000	20	7 000	30
Shareholders' funds:						
Capital issued	5 000		5 000		5 000	
Capital surplus	1 000		1 000		1 000	
Earned surplus	2 000		5 000		5 000	
	8 000	50	11 000	55	11 000	48
Total	16 000	100	20 000	100	23 000	100

CHECK	FRAME	YOUR ANSWER

22. Now in the following year, 1984, Company A continued to expand.

As more funds were clearly needed to finance this expansion, the management considered various ways of acquiring extra funds. They also considered the relative costs involved.

The table for Company A on the opposite page, which adds the liabilities at the end of 1984 to the previous table, shows how the management acquired the extra finance that was needed for the expansion of the company.

Between December 1983 and December 1984 extra finance was acquired by increasing the _____ _____.

22
fixed liabilities

23. In December 1982 the solvency ratio was _____ per cent.

In December 1983 the solvency ratio was _____ per cent.

In December 1984 the solvency ratio was _____ per cent.

23
50
55
48

24. In other words, between 1982 and 1984 the solvency ratio of Company A first [increased/decreased] and then [increased/decreased].

Throughout the period, however, the company was [expanding/contracting].

24
increased
decreased
expanding

25. Expansion of activities, then, can either _____ or _____ the solvency ratio.

CHECK	FRAME	YOUR ANSWER

25
increase
decrease

	COMPANY B *LIABILITIES*				
	Dec. 1982			Dec. 1983	
	Units	%		Units	%
Current liabilities	5 000	25		4 000	25
Fixed liabilities	4 000	20		4 000	25
Shareholders' funds:					
Capital issued	6 000			6 000	
Earned surplus	5 000			2 000	
	11 000	55		8 000	50
Total	20 000	100		16 000	100

26. Now consider Company B. This is a failing company; its activities are decreasing. In 1983 there was a trading loss, and the declining activity resulted in a change in the current liabilities. The table above shows the liabilities for 1982 and 1983 (in units and in percentages).

Now, between December 1982 and December 1983 the company's total finance [increased/decreased]. The current liabilities [increased/decreased] and the trading loss resulted in a decrease in the _____ _____. The solvency ratio _____ from _____ per cent to _____ per cent.

26
decreased
decreased
earned surplus
decreased
55
50

27. In this particular case, then, a decrease in the solvency ratio accompanied [expansion/contraction] of activities.

CHECK	FRAME	YOUR ANSWER

27
contraction

COMPANY B
LIABILITIES

	Dec. 1982		Dec. 1983		Dec. 1984	
	Units	%	Units	%	Units	%
Current liabilities	5 000	25	4 000	25	2 000	16
Fixed liabilities	4 000	20	4 000	25	4 000	32
Shareholders' funds:						
Capital issued	6 000		6 000		6 000	
Earned surplus	5 000		2 000		500	
	11 000	55	8 000	50	6 500	52
Total	20 000	100	16 000	100	12 500	100

---

28. Now, the next year Company B continued to decline. There was a further trading loss and a further general decline in activities. The table above adds the liabilities at December 1984 to the previous table.

In December 1982 the solvency ratio was _____ per cent.

In December 1983 the solvency ratio was _____ per cent.

In December 1984 the solvency ratio was _____ per cent.

In other words, during this period it is clear that the solvency ratio first [decreased/increased], then [decreased/increased].

28
55
50
52
decreased
increased

29. Throughout the period, however, it is evident that the company was [expanding/contracting].

CHECK	FRAME	YOUR ANSWER

| 29
contracting | **30.** To sum up, a contraction of business activity may result in either ....in the solvency ratio. | |

| 30
an increase or a
decrease | **31.** Similarly, an _____ of business activity may result in either an increase or a decrease in the _____ _____. | |

31
expansion
solvency ratio

COMPANY C
LIABILITIES

	Dec. 1983		Dec. 1984	
	Units	%	Units	%
Current liabilities:				
Bank overdraft	6 000		–	
Other	4 000		4 000	
	10 000	28	4 000	12
Fixed liabilities	12 000	34	12 000	34
Shareholders' funds:				
Capital issued	10 000		16 000	
Earned surplus	3 000		3 000	
	13 000	38	19 000	54
Total	35 000	100	35 000	100

32. A change in the solvency ratio, then, may indicate a change in the degree of activity of an enterprise. On the other hand, the solvency ratio may change as a result of a change in the financial structure of an enterprise.

In December 1983 Company C had a bank overdraft at a rate of interest higher than the average rate of dividends paid to shareholders. The table above shows the liabilities of Company C for 1983 and 1984, in units and percentages.

In this case, the total finance [changed/did not change] between December 1983 and December 1984.

CHECK	FRAME	YOUR ANSWER

32
did not change

33. The solvency ratio _____ from _____ per cent to _____ per cent.
  This increase in the solvency ratio resulted from two things: a decrease of _____ (figures) in the _____ liabilities, and an increase of _____ (figures) in the _____ _____ .

33
increased
38, 54
6,000
current
6,000
shareholders' funds
(*or* capital issued)

34. In other words, between December 1983 and December 1984 the company issued more _____ and paid off its _____ _____ .

34
capital
bank overdraft

35. This meant that the company had to pay no _____ on bank overdraft; on the other hand it had to pay _____ to more shareholders.

35
interest
dividends

36. The rate of interest on the overdraft, however, was higher than the average dividend rate. Therefore the action of the management in reducing the current liabilities and increasing the capital issued meant that the overall cost of the company's finance was [increased/reduced].

36
reduced

37. Finally, think this over: high gearing is associated with [high/low] owners' equity.

37
low

38. Low gearing is associated with high owners' equity and [high/low] risk, because a company can easily borrow more money.

CHECK	FRAME	YOUR ANSWER
38 low	**39.** High financial risk relates to [high/low] gearing, because it is difficult to borrow more money when existing liabilities already exceed _____ funds.	
39 high shareholders'	**40.** With high gearing the owners' equity is [high/low] and the outside liabilities are [high/low].	
40 low high	That completes another set. Now note the time you took and the number of frames in which you made a mistake. We are now well over half-way through the programme. Perhaps you should read all the summaries again to convince yourself how much you are learning. Then go on to the next set.	

5. SET 11. LIQUIDITY

Estimated time: 20 minutes

Summary

The current ratio and the quick ratio are two measures of liquidity:

current ratio = current assets : current liabilities
quick ratio = quick assets : current liabilities

The current ratio measures *general* liquidity but the quick ratio measures *immediate* liquidity.

If the current ratio is *lower* than 1 : 1 (e.g. 0.5 : 1, which can also be expressed as 1 : 2), current liabilities exceed current assets. This generally shows that there is a high financial risk because, in business, cash is more important than profit.

If the current ratio is too high (perhaps 3 : 1 or more) this may mean that the company has more money than it can efficiently use. There is no hard and fast rule about a ratio being too high, but when it rises continually over time the situation should be examined.

CHECK	FRAME	YOUR ANSWER
Is your answer right? Check below.	**1.** A company or business enterprise will have to meet its current liabilities in the [short/long] term; it is important, therefore, that there should be enough _____ assets to cover the current liabilities.	
1 short current	**2.** A company is said to be liquid if its current assets exceed its current liabilities. The liquidity of an enterprise is thus a measure of its ability to meet its _____ liabilities out of its current _____.	
2 current assets	**3.** If a company cannot meet its current liabilities from its current assets then it is not _____.	
3 liquid	**4.** Now, an enterprise can be liquid to a greater or lesser degree. There are two ratios which provide useful measures of the degree of liquidity of a company or business enterprise. These are the current ratio and the quick ratio. They are both measures of _____.	
4 liquidity	**5.** The current ratio and the quick ratio are both measures of liquidity, in other words, they are _____ of the company's ability to meet its current liabilities.	
5 measures	**6.** The current ratio indicates to what extent the enterprise can meet its current _____ out of its current assets.	
6 liabilities	**7.** The quick ratio indicates to what extent the enterprise can meet its _____ liabilities out of its quick assets.	

CHECK	FRAME	YOUR ANSWER

7
current

8. Remember that the quick assets are part of the current assets. They are cash and those assets which can be _____ converted into cash. They [do/do not] include stocks (inventories).

8
quickly
do not

9. The relationship between current assets and current _____ and between quick _____ and current liabilities could be expressed as percentages, but in accounting practice they are normally expressed as ratios, e.g. 2 : 1.

9
liabilities
assets

10. Current ratio = $\dfrac{\text{current assets}}{\text{current} \rule{1cm}{0.4pt}}$: 1

10
liabilities

11. Quick ratio = $\dfrac{\text{quick} \rule{1cm}{0.4pt}}{\text{current liabilities}}$: 1

11
assets

COMPANY D

Balance sheet at 31 December 1984
(expressed in WCU)

ASSETS		LIABILITIES	
Quick assets	1 000	Current liabilities	1 000
Inventories	2 000	Fixed liabilities	5 000
Fixed assets	8 000	Shareholders' funds	5 000
Total	11 000	Total	11 000

12. From the simple balance sheet above, calculate the current ratio:

Current ratio = $\dfrac{\text{current} \rule{1cm}{0.4pt}}{\rule{1cm}{0.4pt} \text{ liabilities}}$: 1

$= \dfrac{1,000 + 2,000}{1,000}$: 1 = 3 : 1

CHECK	FRAME	YOUR ANSWER

12
assets
current

13. Referring back to the balance sheet in the previous frame:

$$\text{Quick ratio} = \frac{\underline{\quad\quad} \text{ assets}}{\underline{\quad\quad} \text{ liabilities}} : 1$$

$$= \frac{1,000}{1,000} : 1 = 1 : 1$$

13
quick
current

14. The quick ratio and the _____ _____ are measures of _____. They are both concerned with an enterprise's ability to meet its _____ _____.

14
current ratio
liquidity
current liabilities

15. The current ratio indicates the ability to meet _____ _____ out of _____ _____; the quick ratio indicates the ability to meet current liabilities out of

_____ _____.

15
current liabilities
current assets
quick assets

16. Now let us return to the balance sheet on *Panel E*, and work out the current ratio for Household Utensils Ltd. in 1983 and 1984. To get the current ratio, we divide the _____ _____ by the current liabilities, and to get the quick ratio we divide the quick assets by the

_____ _____.

16
current assets
current liabilities
(*In each case, divide by the current liabilities.*)

17. Fill in the words:

$$\text{Current ratio} = \frac{\overline{\underline{\quad\quad\quad}}}{\underline{\quad\quad\quad}} : 1$$

$$\text{Quick ratio} = \frac{\overline{\underline{\quad\quad\quad}}}{\underline{\quad\quad\quad}} : 1$$

17
current assets
current liabilities
quick assets
current liabilities

18. In December 1983 the current ratio was:

$$\frac{\underline{\quad\quad}\text{(figures)}}{\underline{\quad\quad}\text{(figures)}} = 1.88 : 1$$

CHECK	FRAME	YOUR ANSWER
18 335,400 178,860	**19.** In December 1984 the current ratio is: $$\dfrac{\text{\_\_\_\_\_ (figures)}}{\text{\_\_\_\_\_ (figures)}} = 3.22 : 1$$	
19 267,000 82,974	**20.** In 1983 the quick ratio was: $$\dfrac{\text{\_\_\_\_\_} + \text{\_\_\_\_\_ (figures)}}{\text{\_\_\_\_\_ (figures)}} = 1.42 : 1$$	
20 250 253,850 178,860	**21.** In 1984 the quick ratio is: $$\dfrac{\text{\_\_\_\_\_} + \text{\_\_\_\_\_ (figures)}}{\text{\_\_\_\_\_ (figures)}} = 2.17 : 1$$	
21 450 179,550 82,974	**22.** In 1984 the current ratio is [higher/lower] than in 1983, and in 1984 the quick ratio is [higher/lower] than in 1983.	
22 higher higher	**23.** This means that in 1984 the company had a relatively greater excess of current assets over _____ _____ and also a relatively greater excess of _____ _____ over _____ _____.	
23 current liabilities quick assets current liabilities	**24.** The current ratio is a particularly important measure of the _____ of a business enterprise, and we go on now to consider some of the things it can tell us about the state of a company's finances.	
24 liquidity	**25.** If the current ratio happens to be exactly 1 : 1, this means that the value of the current assets [equals/does not equal] the value of the current liabilities.	

CHECK	FRAME	YOUR ANSWER
25 equals	**26.** If the current ratio is lower than 1 : 1 (e.g. 0·8 : 1), this means that the _____ _____ are greater than the _____ _____.	
26 current liabilities current assets	**27.** As a general rule, it is dangerous to let the current liabilities exceed the current assets, because the company might be unable	
27 to meet its obligations *(or similar words)*	**28.** If the current ratio is above 1, this means that the _____ _____ are greater than the _____ _____.	
28 current assets current liabilities	**29.** Now some current assets can be converted into _____ less easily than others.	
29 cash	**30.** Therefore, in order to feel confident about meeting current liabilities at short notice, a sensible management will make sure that the current assets are _____ than the current liabilities.	
30 greater	**31.** In other words, the current ratio should generally be _____ than 1 : 1. On the other hand, if the current ratio is as high as 3 : 1, this may suggest that the finances of the company need to be reorganised.	
31 higher	**32.** A current ratio of 3 : 1 means that the value of the _____ _____ is three times greater than the value of the _____ _____.	

CHECK	FRAME	YOUR ANSWER

32
current assets
current liabilities

33. A great excess of current assets over current liabilities may mean that a company has more finance than it needs and is putting its excess money into unnecessary current _____ .

33
assets

34. The company may, for instance, be holding too much _____ in the banks.

34
cash

35. Again, for example, the company may be tying up its excess money in large stocks of raw materials, etc., or in giving long credits to its customers.

If the current ratio is very high, then, this may be because the company has too much _____ available.

35
finance *or* money

36. In other words, the company has more _____ than it can use efficiently.

36
finance

ASSETS		LIABILITIES	
Current assets	14 000	Current liabilities (average interest: 1 per cent)	2 000
Fixed assets	18 000	Fixed liabilities (interest: 8 per cent)	13 000
		Shareholders' funds (dividend: 10 per cent)	17 000
Total	32 000	Total	32 000

37. There are other reasons why a high current ratio may indicate a need for a financial reorganisation. Look at the above table of assets and liabilities, for example.

In this case the current ratio is found from the formula: $\dfrac{\text{_____ (figure)}}{\text{_____ (figure)}}$

which gives a ratio of _____ : 1.

CHECK	FRAME	YOUR ANSWER

37	**38.** In this particular case the company is able to make use of all its finances. But the high current ratio still reflects an unsatisfactory situation. Consider how the company has obtained its finances.	
14,000		
2,000		
7		
	It has a relatively [small/large] amount of current liabilities at [high/low] interest rates. It has a [small/large] amount of fixed liabilities and shareholders' money at [high/low] cost.	

38	**39.** In other words the company has acquired too much [cheap/expensive] finance, and has not acquired enough [cheap/expensive] finance.	
small		
low		
large		
high		

39	**40.** In this case, then, the company cannot take advantage of the cheap short-term finance available because it has raised too much expensive permanent and _____ - _____ finance.	
expensive		
cheap		

| 40 | **41.** There are various other reasons why the current ratio may be high. If a company's current ratio rises over a period, then the situation needs to be examined. It may be, however, that there are special circumstances which justify a high current _____. | |
| long-term | | |

| 41 | And that brings us to the end of Chapter 5. Note the time you took and the number of frames in which you made a mistake before reading the summary for this set once more. Do the mini-test and then go on to the next chapter. | |
| ratio | | |

MINI-TEST ON CHAPTER 5

Now, how much have you remembered about this chapter as a whole? As usual, do all the questions below and then check your answers.

1 Here is a table of assets and liabilities. What is the solvency ratio?
_____ per cent.

ASSETS	%	LIABILITIES	%
Current assets	48	Current liabilities	30
Fixed assets	52	Fixed liabilities	34
		Shareholders' funds	36
Total assets	100	Total liabilities	100

2 The solvency ratio indicates how easily an enterprise can meet its _____ _____ out of its _____ _____.

3 The solvency ratio also indicates the proportion of _____ _____ in the _____ _____.

	31 Dec. 1983		31 Dec. 1984	
	Units	%	Units	%
Current liabilities				
Bank overdraft	6 000		4 000	
Others	4 000		_____	
	10 000	28	4 000	12
Fixed liabilities	12 000	34	12 000	34
Shareholders' funds:				
Capital issued	10 000		16 000	
Earned surplus	3 000		3 000	
	13 000	38	19 000	54
Total	35 000	100	35 000	100

4 This table of liabilities shows that the solvency ratio [increased/decreased] from _____ per cent in December 1983 to _____ per cent in December 1984.

Answers to mini-test on Chapter 5

1   36.

2   outside liabilities; total assets.

3   shareholders' funds; total finance (*or* total liabilities).

4   increased; 38; 54.

Mini-test (cont.)

5   An increased solvency ratio:
    (1) always indicates that the enterprise is expanding;
    (2) may result from either expansion or contraction of the
       business.
    Indicate whether you think (1) or (2) correct. _____.

6   Look at the table of liabilities again. What are two reasons for the
    change in the solvency ratio? ....

7   The current ratio and the quick ratio are measures of _____.

8   The current ratio indicates the ability to meet _____ _____ out of
    _____ _____.

9   The quick ratio indicates the ability to meet _____ _____ out of
    _____ _____.

10 Current ratio = $\dfrac{\overline{}}{\overline{}\ \ \overline{}}$: 1 (Fill in the correct words.)

11 Quick ratio = $\dfrac{\overline{}}{\overline{}\ \ \overline{}}$: 1 (Fill in the correct words.)

12 If the current ratio = 1 : 1 this means that _____ _____ = _____
    _____.

13 It is dangerous for the current ratio to be lower than _____. The
    current ratio [should/should not] be higher than 1 : 1.

14 If the current ratio is very high this may mean that the _____ of the
    enterprise should be reorganised. A high current ratio may mean that
    an enterprise has too much _____ available.

15 Another reason for a high current ratio could be that the enter-
    prise has too much [cheap/expensive] finance and not enough
    [cheap/expensive] finance. The [current/quick] ratio gives the best
    indication of ability to meet current liabilities at short notice.

Answers (cont.)

5 (2).

6 Current liabilities have decreased and shareholders' funds have increased; *or* more capital has been issued and bank overdraft has been paid off.

7 liquidity.

8 current liabilities; current assets.

9 current liabilities; quick assets.

10 $\dfrac{\text{current assets}}{\text{current liabilities}}$

11 $\dfrac{\text{quick assets}}{\text{current liabilities}}$

12 current assets; current liabilities.

13 1 : 1; should.

14 finances; finance *or* money.

15 expensive; cheap; quick.

Mini-test (cont.)

Now pull out *Panel X* (page 93) and answer the following questions about the liquidity of Steel Products Ltd. as at 31 December 1984.

16 In December 1983 the current ratio was $\dfrac{\rule{3cm}{0.4pt}}{\rule{2cm}{0.4pt}} = 1.48 : 1$

17 In December 1984 the current ratio was $\dfrac{\rule{3cm}{0.4pt}}{\rule{2cm}{0.4pt}} = 1.60 : 1$

18 In December 1983 the quick ratio was $\dfrac{\rule{1.5cm}{0.4pt} + \rule{1.5cm}{0.4pt}}{\rule{2cm}{0.4pt}} = .74 : 1$

19 In December 1984 the quick ratio was $\dfrac{\rule{1.5cm}{0.4pt} + \rule{1.5cm}{0.4pt}}{\rule{2cm}{0.4pt}} = .64 : 1$

20 From these quick ratios we can see that the _____ _____ were not covered by the _____ _____ in either December 1983 or December 1984.

Answers (cont.)

16 1983: $\dfrac{23,609}{15,974}$

17 1984: $\dfrac{23,727}{14,874}$

18 1983: $\dfrac{191 + 11,626}{15,974}$

19 1984: $\dfrac{190 + 9,373}{14,874}$

20 current liabilities; quick assets.

How did you manage this time?

More than 15 correct?	Very good. You are ready to start Chapter 6.
10-15 correct?	Quite good (especially if you got 14 or 15). But read through the summaries of Sets 10 and 11 before proceeding further.
Fewer than 10 correct?	Take a good break before starting Chapter 5 again.

PROFITABILITY   6

6. SET 12. THE PROFIT AND LOSS ACCOUNT

Estimated time: 20 minutes

Summary

A balance sheet shows assets and how they are financed at a particular date; it needs to be supplemented by a document showing *activity*: sales, costs, profit or loss made during the financial year to the date of the balance sheet. Such a document, which is usually attached to the balance sheet, is known as a profit and loss account (or income statement).

Four different types of profit are given in the profit and loss account: gross profit, operating profit, profit before tax, and net profit after tax.

A company generally gets profits from the sale of goods and services. Some of this money, however, has to be spent on raw materials, wages and factory overhead costs for producing the goods and services. The difference between the money received from sales and the costs directly involved in producing the items sold (the cost of sales) is known as the gross profit.
Thus: *sales − cost of sales = gross profit (GP)*.

Additional expenses are incurred in running the business enterprise as a whole, e.g. office staff, stationery, telephone charges, sales force, and so on; these are termed "operating expenses".
Thus: *gross profit − operating expenses = operating profit (OP)*.

A business may incur further expenses not directly connected with its day-to-day operations, e.g. interest payments on loans, purchase of goodwill, losses on the sale of investments and fixed assets, etc. These are termed "non-operating expenses".
Thus: *operating profit − non-operating expenses = profit before tax (PBT)*.

Income tax must be paid on the profits of a company in most countries; this further reduces the final amount of profit which is available for distribution to the shareholders as dividends or which is retained in the company and carried over as earned surplus.
Thus: *profit before tax − income tax = net profit (net income, net earnings)*.

▶

A separate statement, the statement of earned surplus (or retained earnings), records the earned surplus brought forward, plus the net profit for the year, less the dividends paid. The balance is the figure for earned surplus which is carried forward to the next year on the balance sheet. Any other charges noted in this statement of earned surplus must be investigated and are probably explained in the notes to the financial statements.

CHECK	FRAME	YOUR ANSWER
Is your answer right? Check below.	**1.** Companies are in business to make profits. The most useful overall measure of the condition of a _____ is therefore its profitability.	
1 company	**2.** The profitability of an enterprise is the relationship between the _____ made and the total finance employed to make that profit.	
2 profit	**3.** A balance sheet is a statement of what a company _____ and what it _____ at a particular point in time. It [gives/does not give] a clear statement of the profit made during the year.	
3 owns owes does not give	**4.** Therefore, to assess profitability during any year we need, in addition to the balance sheet, details about the _____ made during the year.	
4 profit	**5.** Most companies provide information about the profit they have made during the year in a document attached to the balance sheet, called the profit and loss account (or income statement). Are a balance sheet and a profit and loss account the same thing? _____.	
5 No	**6.** The total assets and liabilities are constantly changing, so the _____ _____ must be a statement about what these totals are on a particular day.	
6 balance sheet	**7.** The profit and _____ account is very different. It summarises the company's operations and the profit (if any) it has made, during a period of time (usually a year). It [is/is not] a statement of the position on one particular day.	

CHECK	FRAME	YOUR ANSWER
7 loss is not	**8.** A balance sheet will be given a heading like "Balance sheet at 31 December 1983". 　A _____ and _____ account, on the other hand, will be headed "for the year ended 31 December 1983" (or "for the six months ended 30 June 1984").	
8 profit loss	**9.** Would we find a profit and loss account headed "at 31 December 1983"? _____.	
9 No *(It would be given a heading like "for the year ended 31 December 1983.)*	**10.** In this set we shall examine the _____ and loss account briefly before going on in the next set to see how we use the information it contains to compute measures of profitability of a business enterprise.	
10 profit	Open out *Panel F* at page 140 before continuing. **11.** Panel F gives the profit and loss _____ provided by Household Utensils Ltd. with its balance sheet dated 31 December 1984 *(Panel E)*.	
11 account	**12.** This account shows us clearly how _____ were made during 1983 and _____, and what happened to them.	
12 profits 1984	**13.** The primary source of all profits is in goods or services actually sold. Finished products completed during the financial year but not actually sold [do/do not] contribute to profits in that year.	

CHECK	FRAME	YOUR ANSWER
13 do not	**14.** Obviously, not all of the money received from sales is profit, since the goods cost something to make. The amount of money received from sales less the amount spent in producing the goods sold (the cost of sales) = gross _____.	
14 profit	**15.** From the profit and loss account on *Panel F* we can see that Household Utensils Ltd. [increased/decreased] its gross profit from 1983 to 1984.	
15 decreased	**16.** Expenses directly involved in producing the goods sold (such as the cost of raw materials and the wages of the workforce producing the goods) make up the cost of _____.	
16 sales	**17.** Apart from the expenses directly involved in producing the items sold (the _____ of sales), a company is involved in many other expenses in keeping its day-to-day operations running. For example, it may have a team of salesmen, probably an office staff, and almost certainly routine office expenses (stationery, postage, telephones, etc.). All these operating expenses must be paid for out of the gross _____.	
17 cost profit	**18.** The money left out of the gross profit once operating _____ have been paid is referred to as the operating profit.	
18 expenses	**19.** Gross profit – _____ _____ = _____ profit.	

CHECK	FRAME	YOUR ANSWER
19 operating expenses operating	**20.** To summarise what we have said so far: when we subtract the cost of _____ and operating _____ from the total income derived from sales, we have the company's operating profit.	
20 sales expenses	**21.** Look again at *Panel F* and note how the operating profit of Household Utensils Ltd. has _____ from 1983 to 1984.	
21 increased	**22.** Gross profits have _____ but operating profits have increased. This is because the company's _____ _____ have decreased substantially from 1983 to 1984.	
22 decreased operating expenses	**23.** However, to stay in business, the company must meet expenses over and above those directly involved in producing the goods sold and in keeping its plant and machinery operating. In other words, it must meet expenses other than the cost of _____ and _____ expenses.	
23 sales operating	**24.** Because these other expenses do not arise directly from the day-to-day operations of the company, they are described as non-operating _____.	
24 expenses	**25.** Typical examples of expenses not arising directly from a company's day-to-day operations are: interest paid on loans, losses (if any) on the sale of fixed assets and investments, and the purchase of goodwill. These are all examples of non-_____ expenses.	

CHECK	FRAME	YOUR ANSWER
25 operating	**26.** Looking again at *Panel F*, we see that the non-operating expenses of Household Utensils Ltd. [did/did not] increase from 1983 to 1984.	
26 did not	**27.** What were these non-operating expenses and how did they arise? Looking at the profit and loss account on *Panel F* we see that they amounted to _____. Looking at the related balance sheet on *Panel E* we see that the company has to pay interest at 10 per cent per annum on a loan of 50,000 and at _____ per cent per annum on a loan of 8,000.	
27 5,720 9	**28.** Annual interest payable thus equals: $\frac{10 \times 50,000}{100} = 5,000; \frac{9 \times 8,000}{100} = 720;$ $5,000 + 720 =$ _____ = the company's non-operating expenses. (We have already calculated this – see Set 5, frame 34.)	
28 5,720	**29.** When non-operating expenses are deducted from the operating _____, we have the figure for profit before tax. Operating profit – non-operating expenses = profit _____ _____.	
29 profit before tax	**30.** To summarise again what we have said so far: gross profit = sales – cost of _____; operating profit = sales – cost of sales – _____ _____; and _____ before _____ = sales – cost of sales – operating expenses – non-operating expenses.	

CHECK	FRAME	YOUR ANSWER

30
sales
operating expenses
profit
tax

31. In almost every country of the world, companies have to pay tax on the profits they earn. This _____ is only paid some time after the end of the company's financial year, but provision has to be made for it from the profits for that year.

31
tax

32. Tax payable is shown on the balance sheet and on the profit and _____ _____. On both *Panel E* and *Panel F* we see that Household Utensils Ltd. made a provision for taxation of _____ in 1983 and of 3,755 in _____.

32
loss account
2,810
1984

33. Profit before tax − tax = net _____ after _____.

33
profit
tax

STATEMENT OF EARNED SURPLUS
34. The net profit _____ _____ is money available to the company for use as the directors see fit. All of it may be distributed to the owners of the company, the _____, as dividends, although this is very rarely done.

34
after tax
shareholders

35. Most companies are expanding all the time and need extra funds to finance their expansion. Usually some (or even all) of the _____ _____ after tax will be retained in the company to provide at least part of the funds needed to finance the expansion.

35
net profit

36. Profits retained in the company are added to the _____ surplus.

CHECK	FRAME	YOUR ANSWER

36
earned

37. Looking at the statement of earned surplus for 1983 on *Panel F*, we see that 3,000 units of net profit of 8,430 were paid out as _____ to shareholders and the remaining _____ units increased the earned surplus account.

37
dividends
5,430 *(8,430 – 3,000)*

38. In 1984 _____ units were paid out as dividends and 6,266 (11,266 – 5,000) were retained in the company as _____ _____.

38
5,000
earned surplus

39. From the statement of earned surplus on *Panel F* we see that net 5,430 (8,430 – 3,000) units were added to the earned surplus during 1983, and from the balance sheet on *Panel E* we see that the earned surplus at 31 December 1983 was _____. At the end of 1982, therefore, there must have been an earned surplus of 11,300 – 5,430 = _____.

39
.11,300
5,870

40. Since the earned surplus at 31 December 1983 was 11,300 *(Panel E)* and _____ was retained during 1984 *(Panel F)*, earned surplus at the end of 1984 must have been 11,300 + 6,266 = _____, which, as we see from the balance sheet on *Panel E*, was the case.

40
6,266
17,566

That is the end of another set. Note the time you took and the number of frames in which you made a mistake. Then read the summary for this set again, before going on to try Set 13.

6. SET 13. TWO MEASURES OF PROFITABILITY

Estimated time: 20 minutes

Summary

There are two useful measures of the profitability of a business enterprise: return on total investment and return on shareholders' funds; they are usually expressed as percentages:

$$\text{Return on total investment} = \frac{\text{profit before tax} + \text{interest on fixed liabilities} \times 100}{\text{total investment}}$$

$$\text{Return on shareholders' funds} = \frac{\text{net profit after tax} \times 100}{\text{shareholders' funds}}$$

The figures for profit will be obtained from the profit and loss account and the figures for total investment and shareholders' funds from the balance sheet.

Total investment is generally defined as total assets less current liabilities. This is the same as shareholders' funds plus long-term liabilities.

A financial ratio is like the financial "temperature" of a business; it is "healthy" when it complies with normal accepted ratios for the industry which are usually published each year by chambers of commerce, industrial associations or the government.

CHECK	FRAME	YOUR ANSWER

| | **RETURN ON TOTAL INVESTMENT** | |
| Is your answer right? Check below. | **1.** By putting together information from a company's balance sheet for a certain date, and the _____ and _____ account for the year ending on that date, we can calculate the profitability of a business enterprise. | |

| 1 profit loss | **2.** There are various formulas which can be used for this purpose. We shall consider only two: those that give us a measure of "return on total investment" and "return on shareholders' funds". These are both measures of the _____ of a business enterprise. | |

| 2 profitability | **3.** Now, to operate a business and earn profits the management must have the use of permanent and long-term finance. This finance appears on the balance sheet as _____ funds and _____ liabilities. | |

| 3 shareholders' fixed | **4.** The shareholders' _____ and the fixed _____ represent finance invested in the company by shareholders and others. | |

| 4 funds liabilities | **5.** The shareholders' investment (or shareholders' funds) is the money subscribed by the shareholders, plus p_____ retained in the company. | |

| 5 profits | **6.** Profits retained in the company are credited to the shareholders. They are added to the shareholders' funds and can be regarded as part of the shareholders' _____ in the company. | |

CHECK	FRAME	YOUR ANSWER
6 investment	**7.** The _____ liabilities are also investments in the company, but the current liabilities are not investments. The current liabilities represent credit extended to the company on a _____-_____ basis.	
7 fixed short-term	**8.** The total investment in the company, then, is the _____ _____ plus the _____ _____.	
8 shareholders' funds fixed liabilities	**9.** One of the most useful overall measures of profitability is a ratio known as return on total investment. This ratio gives a measure of the management's skill in exploiting the _____ invested in the company.	
9 funds (*or* money)	**10.** Now, return on total investment indicates the relation between the _____ earned and the total investment in the company.	
10 profit	**11.** In other words, the return on _____ investment is the return, or profit, on the _____ _____ plus the _____ _____.	
11 total shareholders' funds fixed liabilities	**12.** The return on total investment is a measure of the skill of the _____ in exploiting the funds made available by the investors.	
12 management	**13.** The general formula for return on total investment is: $$\frac{return}{total\ investment.}$$ Now, we have already seen that total investment is _____ _____ + _____ _____.	

CHECK	FRAME	YOUR ANSWER
13 shareholders' funds fixed liabilities	**14.** Let us now find out what the word "_____" in the top line of this formula means. Remember that this ratio is an overall measure of the skill of the management.	
14 return	**15.** Now, the management has no control over the amount of profits tax that is paid on the profits. Therefore the fairest indication of how profitable the enterprise has been is profit [before/after] tax.	
15 before	**16.** The basic part of the "return" in the formula above, then, is profit _____ _____.	
16 before tax	**17.** Now, the figure for profit before tax is the figure for profit [before/after] dividends are paid to shareholders. (Look at *Panel F* if you are not sure.)	
17 before	**18.** In other words, profit before tax includes compensation to be paid to _____ for their investment.	
18 shareholders	**19.** Now, total investment, remember, means _____ _____ + _____ _____.	
19 shareholders' funds fixed liabilities	**20.** Therefore, if "return" includes compensation to be paid to shareholders it should also include compensation paid on the _____ _____.	
20 fixed liabilities	**21.** In this formula, therefore, "return" should include the i_____ on the fixed liabilities.	

CHECK	FRAME	YOUR ANSWER
21 interest	**22.** Does the figure for profit before tax include the interest on the fixed liabilities? _____. (Look at *Panel F* if you are not sure.)	
22 No	**23.** The interest on the fixed liabilities together with other expenses make up the non-operating expenses which are deducted from the operating profit to arrive at the figure for profit _____ _____. So profit before tax [does/does not] include interest on fixed liabilities.	
23 before tax does not	**24.** But "return" in our formula should include the interest on the fixed liabilities. Therefore, this interest should be added to the profit before tax in calculating the "return". Return = profit before tax + ...	
24 interest on fixed liabilities	**25.** Now, complete the formula for return on total investment which is: $$\frac{\text{return}}{\text{total investment}}$$ where return = profit _____ tax + interest on _____ _____ and total investment = _____ _____ + _____ _____ .	
25 before fixed liabilities shareholders' funds fixed liabilities	**26.** The return on total investment ratio is usually expressed as a percentage: $$\frac{\text{return} \times 100}{\text{total investment}}$$ In other words, _____ before tax + interest on fixed liabilities x 100 is divided by _____ _____ + fixed liabilities.	

Profitability

CHECK	FRAME	YOUR ANSWER
26 profit shareholders' funds	**27.** In working out the return on total investment we can find the figure for profit before tax from the [balance sheet/profit and loss account]. The figures for shareholders' funds and fixed liabilities will come from the _____ _____.	
27 profit and loss account balance sheet	**28.** The remaining figure we will have to find is the _____ on _____ liabilities. Can we always get this figure from the profit and loss account? _____.	
28 interest fixed No *The figure for non-operating expenses includes interest on fixed liabilities but may include other items as well.)*	**29.** You can work out the annual interest on the fixed liabilities, however, from the information given in the _____ _____.	
29 balance sheet	**30.** Look at the balance sheet for our company on *Panel E.* In 1984 the total annual interest on the fixed liabilities is _____ per cent on _____ plus _____ per cent on _____.	
30 10 50,000 9 8,000	**31.** In 1984 the interest on the fixed liabilities is 5,000 + 720 = 5,720. The interest on the fixed liabilities in 1983 was [the same/not the same] as in 1984.	

CHECK	FRAME	YOUR ANSWER

31
the same

32. Look at *Panel E* and *Panel F* and fill in the missing figures below. For 1983 the return on total investment (as a percentage) was:

$$\frac{(\underline{\quad} + \underline{\quad}) \times 100}{\underline{\quad} + \underline{\quad}} = 9.54 \text{ per cent}$$

32
11,240 + 5,720
119,740 + 58,000

33. For 1984 the return on total investment (as a percentage) was:

$$\frac{(\underline{\quad} + \underline{\quad}) \times 100}{\underline{\quad} + \underline{\quad}} = 10.17 \text{ per cent}$$

33
15,021 + 5,720
146,006 + 58,000

34. As shown by the return on total investment, was the company more profitable in 1983 or 1984? _____.

34
1984

35. In other words, the total permanent and long-term funds were employed more _____ by the management in 1984.

35
profitably (*or* effectively)

36. To repeat, the formula for return on total investment is:

$$\frac{\dots\dots + \dots\dots}{\underline{\quad}\ \underline{\quad} + \underline{\quad}\ \underline{\quad}}$$

36
profit before tax + interest on fixed liabilities
shareholders' funds
fixed liabilities

RETURN ON SHAREHOLDERS' FUNDS
37. We have seen that return on total investment is a measure of the return on the shareholders' investment (shareholders' funds) and the long-term investment by other people (fixed liabilities). It is a useful overall measure of the ability of the _____.

CHECK	FRAME	YOUR ANSWER
37 management	**38.** Now, the ordinary shareholders may be particularly interested in the return on their investment: in other words, the return on the ordinary _____ _____ alone.	
38 shareholders' funds	**39.** The return on shareholders' funds (or shareholders' investment) in any one year is the relation between the net profit available for the shareholder and the total shareholders' funds. That is: Net _____ available for _____ shareholders' funds	
39 profit shareholders	**40.** The part of the profit that is paid as tax is obviously not available for the shareholders: "net profit" in the above formula, then, means net profit [before/after] tax.	
40 after	**41.** The figure for profit before tax, on the other hand, is used in working out the return on t_____ _____.	
41 total investment	**42.** Profit before tax is used in working out the return on total investment. In working out the return on the shareholders' funds, "return" means net profit _____ _____.	
42 after tax	**43.** Return on shareholders' funds = return (i.e. ....) shareholders' funds	
43 net profit after tax	**44.** Generally, the figure for net profit after tax [can/cannot] be obtained from the balance sheet.	

CHECK	FRAME	YOUR ANSWER

44
cannot *(but it should be given in the profit and loss account)*

45. Fill in the missing figures below. We are still referring to Household Utensils Ltd. (the balance sheet is on *Panel E*, the profit and loss account on *Panel F*). For 1983 the return on shareholders' funds, as a percentage, was:

$$\frac{\underline{\hspace{2cm}} \times 100}{\underline{\hspace{1.5cm}}} = 7.04 \text{ per cent}$$

45
8,430
119,740

46. For 1984 the return on the shareholders' funds, as a percentage, was:

$$\frac{\underline{\hspace{1.5cm}} \times \underline{\hspace{1.5cm}}}{\underline{\hspace{1.5cm}}} = 7.72 \text{ per cent}$$

46
11,266 × 100
146,006

47. From the shareholders' point of view, then, was the return on investment more satisfactory in 1983 or 1984? _____.

47
1984

48. Ratios are like thermometers which show the financial "temperature" of the business to determine whether it is financially _____ or not.

48
healthy

49. A healthy business today may not be healthy in the future. Thus, we must forecast the future _____ statements and the future ratios.

49
financial

50. Healthy ratios depend upon the normal ratios for the industry which vary over time and also according to the size and type of the business. Normal ratios are published by chambers of commerce or industrial associations or sometimes by the g_____.

CHECK	FRAME	YOUR ANSWER

| 50 government | That is the end of Set 13. Note the time you took and the number of frames in which you made a mistake. Then read the summary for this set again, before going on to Set 14, the shortest set in the book. | |

6. SET 14. THE VALUATION OF AN ENTERPRISE

Estimated time: 10 minutes

Summary

Assessing the value of an enterprise is a complicated procedure. The aim of this set is not to teach you how to value a business, but rather to point out why you *cannot* value a business simply by examining its balance sheet.

A business enterprise can be valued either as a "going concern" or as an enterprise that will be wound up: for either purpose the information on the balance sheet is inadequate.

If the business is to be wound up, we need to know how much cash will be left when the assets have been sold and all the liabilities have been paid. The balance sheet will not help us, because the fixed assets of a going concern are valued at cost less accumulated depreciation; this may be more or less than the realisable market value. Similarly, current assets are valued at cost – or in the case of inventories at cost or market value, whichever is the lower – in the ordinary course of business but *not* on liquidation. Therefore, the balance sheet will not allow us to assess the net worth of an enterprise that is to be wound up.

If the business is to continue as a going concern, the value of its assets will be of less importance than its *future* profitability. In addition to past performance, there are many factors not expressed in terms of money on the balance sheet or profit and loss account that have an enormous effect on the future profitability of the company. Some of these will be discussed in Set 16, the final set.

Overall, the value of a business is determined only when it is actually sold. The sales price may be more or less than the shareholders' funds shown on the latest balance sheet. The value depends on future profitability and on the realisable value of the assets if the business is wound up (the "asset back-up" which prevents the "downside risk" of loss).

CHECK	FRAME	YOUR ANSWER
Is your answer right? Check below.	**1.** We can consider the value of an enterprise from two points of view: its value as a "going concern" (that is, as an enterprise that will continue to operate), or its _____ as an enterprise that will be wound up, or liquidated.	
1 value	**2.** In either case it will be necessary to assess the worth of the enterprise. Net worth is the value of the total assets, less those liabilities that the enterprise is bound to meet. In other words, net worth is total assets, less _____ liabilities and _____ liabilities.	
2 current fixed	**3.** Now suppose that we want to know the value of an enterprise that is to be wound up. First we have to see if we can discover its net worth from the balance sheet. Net worth, remember, means the difference between the _____ _____ and the	
3 total assets current and fixed liabilities (*or* outside liabilities)	**4.** We could look at the values given to the assets and the outside liabilities on the balance sheet. The figures against the outside liabilities will probably be accurate, but what about the values shown for the _____? (Remember that we are concerned with an enterprise that is to be wound up.)	
4 assets	**5.** In the normal course of events, the values shown for the assets on a balance sheet are based on the assumption that the enterprise will [continue to operate as a going concern/be wound up].	

CHECK	FRAME	YOUR ANSWER
5 continue to operate as a going concern	**6.** A balance sheet [does/does not] indicate the "break-up" values of the assets, in other words, what the assets could be sold for if the company ceased operations.	
6 does not	**7.** If an enterprise is to be wound up, then the balance sheet will not give a reasonable indication of the value of the assets. Therefore the balance sheet will not allow us to assess the _____ _____ of an enterprise that is to be wound up.	
7 net worth	**8.** Now, if we wanted to value a going concern (an enterprise that will continue to operate), we would once again need to know the net worth. In other words, we would need to know the value of the ____ ____ less the ____ ____.	
8 total assets outside liabilities	**9.** Would the balance sheet give us a reasonable indication of the value of the assets of a going concern? _____	
9 Yes (*The figures would need some adjustment but would give a reasonable indication.*)	**10.** The balance sheet will also show the outside liabilities. In all normal circumstances, then, the balance sheet will allow us to assess the _____ _____ of a going concern.	
10 net worth	**11.** But, when valuing an enterprise as a going concern it is necessary to consider not only the net worth but also the profitability of the enterprise. In the last set we considered the question of [past/future] profitability.	

CHECK	FRAME	YOUR ANSWER
11 past	**12.** In valuing an enterprise, however, _____ profitability will be more important than past profitability.	
12 future	**13.** In valuing an enterprise as a going concern, then, the two major factors to be considered are _____ _____ and _____ _____.	
13 net worth future profitability	**14.** As we shall discuss in the final set (Set 16), future profitability depends on a great number of factors, including the qualities of the product, the activities of competitors, the general economic situation, and so on. Must we make financial forecasts? _____.	
14 Yes	**15.** It [is/is not] possible to make an accurate assessment of future profitability from a balance sheet.	
15 is not	That is the end of the shortest set in the book. Note the time you took and the number of frames in which you made a mistake. Then read the summary for the set once again before going on to test your knowledge of the whole chapter in the mini-test which follows.	

MINI-TEST ON CHAPTER 6

Answer the questions below and when you have finished check your answers on the Progress Work Sheet.

1 Is it true that the balance sheet tells us all that we need to know about the financial position of a company or business enterprise? _____ .

2 A balance sheet is a statement about certain aspects of a business enterprise's finances *at* a particular point in time, while a profit and loss account is a statement about changes that have taken place _____ a period of time.

3 All the _____ of a company are ultimately derived from goods or services sold.

4 Sales − cost of sales = _____ _____ .

5 Gross profit − operating expenses = _____ _____ .

6 Payment of interest on long-term loans and purchase of goodwill are examples of _____ - _____ _____ a company might have to meet.

7 Operating profit − non-operating expenses = ...

8 Dividends are paid out of a company's net profit _____ _____ .

9 Any of the net profits after tax not used in the payment of dividends will be transferred to _____ _____ .

10 Return on total investment and return on shareholders' funds are measures of an enterprise's profitability. Return on total investment is a useful overall measure of the ability of the _____ .

11 By total investment we mean ....

12 Return on total investment = $\dfrac{.........+.........}{\text{_____ _____} + \text{_____ _____}}$

13 Return on shareholders' funds = $\dfrac{.........}{\text{_____ _____}}$

Answers to mini-test on Chapter 6

1   No.

2   during.

3   profits.

4   gross profit.

5   operating profit.

6   non-operating expenses.

7   profit before tax.

8   after tax.

9   earned surplus.

10 management.

11 shareholders' funds plus fixed liabilities.

12 $\dfrac{\text{profit before tax} + \text{interest on fixed liabilities}}{\text{shareholders' funds} + \text{fixed liabilities}}$

13 $\dfrac{\text{net profit after tax}}{\text{shareholders' funds}}$

Mini-test (cont.)

Open out *Panel Y*: the balance sheet for Steel Products Ltd. at 31 December 1984 and the profit and loss account for 1983 and 1984.

14 Note that the dividends paid to shareholders in 1983 are [greater/less] than the profit after tax for 1983. The dividends will therefore have the effect of _____ the earned surplus which had accumulated by the end of 1982.

15 Now work out which was the more profitable year in terms of the return on total investment. (Finish the job this time and work out the percentages: work them out on a piece of paper.)

$$1983 : \frac{(\underline{\hspace{1cm}} + \underline{\hspace{1cm}}) \times 100}{\underline{\hspace{1cm}} + \underline{\hspace{1cm}}} = \frac{\underline{\hspace{1cm}}}{\underline{\hspace{1cm}}} = \underline{\hspace{1cm}} \text{ per cent.}$$

$$1984 : \frac{(\underline{\hspace{1cm}} + \underline{\hspace{1cm}}) \times 100}{\underline{\hspace{1cm}} + \underline{\hspace{1cm}}} = \frac{\underline{\hspace{1cm}}}{\underline{\hspace{1cm}}} = \underline{\hspace{1cm}} \text{ per cent.}$$

In terms of return on total investment, 1984 was [more/less] profitable than 1983. _____.

16 Now work out for each year the return on shareholders' funds.

$$1983 : \frac{\underline{\hspace{1cm}} \times 100}{\underline{\hspace{1cm}}} = \frac{\underline{\hspace{1cm}}}{\underline{\hspace{1cm}}} = \underline{\hspace{1cm}} \text{ per cent.}$$

$$1984 : \frac{\underline{\hspace{1cm}} \times 100}{\underline{\hspace{1cm}}} = \frac{\underline{\hspace{1cm}}}{\underline{\hspace{1cm}}} = \underline{\hspace{1cm}} \text{ per cent.}$$

In other words, 1984 was [more/less] profitable than 1983 from the shareholders' point of view. _____.

17 When assessing the value of an enterprise, can we include the value of the husband or wife of the accountant who always helps out with the difficult figures? _____.

18 The net worth of an enterprise that is to be wound up [can/cannot] be assessed from the balance sheet.

19 When assessing the value of an enterprise as a going concern we need to know both the net worth and the prospects of _____
_____.

20 Is the following statement correct or incorrect? It is possible to assess the value of an enterprise from the balance sheet alone. _____.

Answers (cont.)

14 greater; reducing.

15 $\dfrac{(601 + 685) \times 100}{25,560 + 13,000} = \dfrac{128,600}{38,560} = 3.3$ per cent

$\dfrac{(3,520 + 460) \times 100}{27,255 + 8,500} = \dfrac{398,000}{35,755} = 11.1$ per cent

More.

16 $\dfrac{508 \times 100}{25,560} = \dfrac{50,800}{25,560} = 1.9$ per cent

$\dfrac{2,892 \times 100}{27,255} = \dfrac{289,200}{27,255} = 10.6$ per cent

More.

17 No (because the value of a good spouse can never be expressed in monetary terms!)

18 cannot.

19 future profitability.

20 Incorrect.

How did you get on?

More than 15 correct?	Excellent! Go on at once to the final chapter.
10-15 correct?	You should read through the summaries of Sets 12, 13 and 14 before going on to the final chapter.
Fewer than 10 correct?	You should take a break and then return to Set 12 again.

ASSESSING
THE BALANCE SHEET **7**

7. SET 15. RELIABILITY

Estimated time: 25 minutes

Summary

A balance sheet offers useful information but how can we determine that the data are reliable? We must check the internal consistency of the balance sheet with the associated financial statements: the profit and loss account, the sources and uses of funds statement, the auditor's certificate and the notes to the financial statements.

The balance sheet and associated financial statements should show:

1. the name of the company and the date. It is important in assessing a company's present financial position to see the *latest* balance sheet – that is, one which is not more than six months old;
2. separate totals for the current and fixed assets and liabilities;
3. the basis on which the assets have been valued;
4. the director's signature, which indicates the acceptance of re-sponsibility for the published figures, and a clear certificate from an independent, professionally qualified auditor.

The balance sheet will probably not show:

1. whether the company, its directors and the auditor have a good reputation;
2. ownership of a company's shares. If a few people own most of the shares they may have great influence on the company, and it may be important to consider their reputation;
3. that the laws of the country in which the company operates have been complied with;
4. the extent to which generally accepted accounting and auditing standards have been modified to comply with tax laws or to produce conservative results.

5. the future operations, profitability and health of the business.

Overall, be cautious before accepting a balance sheet as a "true and fair view" of the company's position. ▶

IMPORTANT NOTE

The key to the balance sheet may often be found in the auditor's certificate and the notes to the financial statements.

CHECK	FRAME	YOUR ANSWER

Is your answer right? Check below.

1. We have to be cautious about accepting a balance sheet as a true statement of a company's assets and _____.

liabilities

2. In this set we are going to look at several ways in which we can get some indication of whether or not a balance _____ is a reliable statement of a company's financial position.

2
sheet

TIMBER PRODUCTS LTD.
Balance sheet

ASSETS		LIABILITIES	
Current assets	3 480	Current liabilities	2 870
Fixed assets	10 490	Fixed liabilities	4 350
		Shareholders' funds	6 750
Total assets	13 970	Total liabilities	13 970

---

3. What should we look for on the balance sheet itself? Up to frame 40 we are going to be concerned with this question.

Look at the very simple balance sheet above. This is not a very informative balance sheet; it gives very little detail. There is also one very important thing missing from it. This is the _____ of the balance sheet.

3
date

4. To assess a company's present financial position it is essential to see its most recent balance sheet. If the balance sheet has no _____ you cannot be sure that it is the most recent one.

153

CHECK	FRAME	YOUR ANSWER

4
date

5. It is equally important, of course, that a balance sheet should give the _____ of the company.

5
name

6. Before you accept a balance sheet, then, make sure that it bears the ....and the _____.

6
name of the
company
date

JOHNSON MANUFACTURING CO. LTD.
Balance sheet at 31 December 1982

ASSETS		LIABILITIES	
Manufacturing tools and stocks of raw materials	18 000	Bank overdraft and mortgage loan	50 600
Land, buildings and marketable securities	80 400	Accounts payable	8 700
Finished products, customers' accounts and goodwill	41 800	Capital issued, earned surplus, and loan from development bank, repayable 1988	80 900
Total assets	140 200	Total liabilities	140 200

---

7. Here is another simple balance sheet. First look at the assets on this balance sheet. The first entry is manufacturing tools and stocks of _____ _____.

7
raw materials

8. Manufacturing tools come under [current/fixed] assets, and stocks of raw materials are _____ assets.

8
fixed
current

9. Now look at the second entry in the assets. Is this also a mixture of current and fixed assets? _____.

CHECK	FRAME	YOUR ANSWER
es	**10.** The current assets in the second item are the _____ _____.	
0 narketable ecurities	**11.** In the third entry under assets there are two current assets and one fixed asset. Which is the fixed asset? _____.	
1 Goodwill	**12.** By looking at this list of assets, is it possible to work out the value of the current assets? _____.	
2 No	**13.** A balance sheet should always be set out in such a way that it is possible to work out the separate totals of the _____ assets and the _____ assets.	
3 urrent xed	**14.** Now look at the liabilities on the balance sheet in frame 7. Would you say that these are set out in the clearest possible way? _____.	
4 No	**15.** Look at the first entry under liabilities. Bank overdrafts are _____ liabilities, and mortgage loans are _____ liabilities.	
5 urrent xed	**16.** Look at the third entry under liabilities. Capital issued and earned surplus are part of the _____ _____; the long-term development bank loan is a _____ liability.	
6 nareholders' funds xed	**17.** By looking at this list of liabilities, could you tell the amount of the shareholders' funds? _____. Could you work out the total current liabilities? _____.	

CHECK	FRAME	YOUR ANSWER
17 No No	**18.** If you saw a balance sheet set out like the one in frame 7, would you accept it without question as a document that would allow you to make a reliable assessment of a company's position? _____.	
18 No	**19.** Look at the assets again. Can you tell on what basis they have been valued? _____.	
19 No	**20.** A reliable balance sheet will always indicate the basis of the _____ of the assets.	
20 valuation *(The basis of valuation may be shown on the balance sheet or on notes attached.)*	**21.** Fixed assets are normally valued at _____ less _____.	
21 cost depreciation	**22.** Current assets in the form of stocks of materials and finished products are normally valued at	
22 cost or market value, whichever is the lower	**23.** Current assets in the form of marketable securities are normally valued at _____, but the _____ _____ should also be stated.	
23 cost market value	**24.** Customers' accounts are _____ assets. On the balance sheet the value of the customers' accounts is [sometimes/never] reduced to allow for predicted "bad debts".	

CHECK	FRAME	YOUR ANSWER
24 current (*or* quick) sometimes	**25.** The balance sheet (or the notes attached) should always make clear the _____ of the _____ of the assets.	
25 basis valuation	**26.** It is also important that assets should be valued on a constant basis from year to year. If the same assets are valued on one basis at one date and on another basis at another date, it is difficult to _____ the company's position at the two dates.	
26 compare	**27.** Assets, then, should always be valued on a _____ basis. Otherwise, it is _____ to compare a company's position at different dates.	
27 constant difficult	**28.** Before we finish looking at the balance sheet in frame 7, suppose that you are assessing the company's position in 1984. If you were shown this balance sheet, would you accept it as the most recent balance sheet the company could produce? _____.	
28 No	**29.** Why would you not accept this balance sheet as the most recent one?	
29 Because it is dated December 1982	**30.** To sum up so far, you can begin to decide whether a balance sheet is acceptable by examining the balance sheet itself. The first thing to check is that it gives the _____ of the company and the _____ of the balance sheet.	

CHECK	FRAME	YOUR ANSWER
30 name date	**31.** Secondly, look to see whether the balance sheet is set out clearly. It should be possible to work out separately the values of the different classes of _____ and _____.	
31 assets liabilities	**32.** Thirdly, if you are comparing the balance sheets of an enterprise at different dates, make sure that the assets are valued on a _____ basis.	
32 constant	**33.** The _____ on which the assets are valued should always be indicated on a balance sheet (or on notes attached). If the assets have not been valued according to the usual basis you may need to inquire why this is so.	
33 basis	**34.** Now, in deciding whether the balance sheet of a limited liability company can be accepted without question as a reliable statement, there are two other things you should look for on the balance sheet itself. First, the directors of a limited liability company are responsible for the preparation of the balance sheet, and they must sign the balance sheet to show that they accept this _____.	
34 responsibility	**35.** You should always make sure that a limited company's balance sheet has been signed by one or more of the _____.	
35 directors	**36.** The balance sheet of a limited company should be accepted with caution if it has not been _____ by one or more of the _____.	

CHECK	FRAME	YOUR ANSWER
36 signed directors	**37.** Secondly, look on the balance sheet for a certificate from the auditor. The balance sheet of every limited company must be examined by an independent examiner (auditor). The _____ then certifies that the balance sheet shows a true and fair picture of the company's position.	
37 auditor	**38.** Always make sure, then, that a balance sheet bears a clear _____ from the auditor.	
38 certificate	**39.** The auditor is free to make comments about the figures shown on the balance sheet whether in the auditor's certificate or by requiring additional notes to financial statements. Therefore, always read the _____ certificate carefully.	
39 auditor's	**40.** A balance sheet should be treated with great caution if it is not _____ by one or more of the directors or if there is no certificate from the _____. What about an auditor who is the manager's uncle? _____.	
40 signed auditor No *(an auditor should be independent)*.	**41.** So far we have noted the things we need to look for on the balance sheet itself in order to determine whether or not it is a _____ statement.	
41 reliable	**42.** But there are other factors which do not appear on the _____ sheet that also need to be taken into account.	

CHECK	FRAME	YOUR ANSWER

42
balance

43. Suppose you are looking at a certain balance sheet.

It gives the name of the company, and it is dated.

It is clearly set out, it lists the different classes of assets and liabilities separately, and it indicates how the assets have been valued.

It is signed by two directors and the auditor's certificate is attached; the auditor has not expressed any reservations about the figures.

The balance sheet is properly printed and looks impressive.

On the basis of this evidence alone, could you be certain that the balance sheet is a reliable statement? _____.

43
No

44. In addition to what is shown on the balance sheet, you have to consider factors *outside* the balance sheet before you can be sure that it presents a reliable picture.

Study also the profit and loss account, the sources and uses of funds statement and the notes to the financial statements. Consider the factor of *reputation*. If the company concerned has a long-established _____ for honesty and efficiency, you can be fairly confident about accepting its balance sheet.

44
reputation

45. Again, you can be fairly confident about accepting a balance sheet if you know that:
(*a*) the _____ who has examined and certified it is properly qualified and has a good reputation; and
(*b*) the _____ who have signed it have a good reputation.

CHECK	FRAME	YOUR ANSWER
45 auditor directors	**46.** In other words, when deciding whether a company's balance sheet can be accepted as giving a reliable picture you may have to consider the reputation of the _____, the _____, and the _____ itself.	
46 auditor directors company	**47.** In some cases, the ownership of a company's shares may also be important. If most of the shares are owned by a very small number of shareholders, these people will probably have a great deal of influence in the company, and it may therefore be important to consider their _____.	
47 reputation	**48.** If the company, the directors and the auditor all have a high reputation, you can probably assume that the law of the country has been complied with. Many countries have _____ designed to control company operations generally, and various aspects of balance sheets in particular.	
48 laws	**49.** For example, the law of the country may specify the basis of the valuation of _____. The law may also control the rate at which fixed assets can be _____, or reduced in value.	
49 assets depreciated	**50.** In some countries, companies are also obliged by law to put some of their annual net profit into a "legal reserve". This reserve is part of the _____ funds, but can be used only for purposes laid down by _____.	

CHECK	FRAME	YOUR ANSWER
50 shareholders' law	**51.** Normally, a balance sheet cannot be accepted as a satisfactory statement of a company's affairs unless it satisfies the _____ of the country.	
51 law	**52.** To sum up, when you are deciding whether a particular balance sheet is likely to be a reliable statement of a company's affairs, you have to consider factors shown on the balance sheet and also factors	
52 not shown on the balance sheet	You will soon be reaching the end of the book. Note the time you took to complete this set and the number of frames in which you made a mistake. Then read the summary for this set once again before going on to the final set.	

7.   SET 16. LIMITATIONS

Estimated time: 20 minutes

Summary

When we are making any assessment of a company's position, we must be aware that the balance sheet can give only a limited picture of the company's state of affairs. The greatest limitation of the information contained on a balance sheet is that it is concerned *only* with things that can be expressed in monetary terms.

A company's present financial position (as reflected in its latest balance sheet) is important in determining its future potential. Equally important, however, are factors such as the nature of the company's products (especially in relation to expected technological developments), the skill and morale of management and staff, the activities of competitors, and general economic conditions. Such information must be taken into account along with the balance sheet figures in assessing the future prospects of a business enterprise.

The balance sheet is also limited because the figures which appear on it are only estimates and not scientific facts. The key accounting concept is not absolute accuracy but rather materiality; it is very difficult to value assets exactly. Furthermore, unless special inflation accounting techniques are adopted (see the technical note in Appendix A), a balance sheet assumes that the value of money remains unchanged over time, which is certainly not true.

Overall, be cautious, not only, as we stressed in the previous set, before accepting a balance sheet as reliable but also before using the information contained on it as an indication of the future performance of a business enterprise.

Always study carefully the profit and loss account, the sources and uses of funds statement, the notes to the financial statements and the auditor's certificate. Determine if the auditor was professionally qualified, independent, and adequately paid to complete a professional audit; check that the auditor was able to complete the audit within six months of the end of the financial year.

CHECK	FRAME	YOUR ANSWER
Is your answer right? Check below.	**1.** Perhaps the most obvious limitation of the balance sheet is that it gives an incomplete picture of the state of affairs of a company. It will always give an incomplete picture because it is concerned only with factors that can be expressed in _____ terms.	
1 monetary	**2.** For example, the fact that a company has a number of strong competitors may be a very important aspect of its position; but this would never be indicated on the _____ _____.	
2 balance sheet	**3.** Similarly, the company may be producing a product which will soon be rendered old-fashioned, or even obsolete, by technological developments. This too [would/would not] be reflected on the balance sheet.	
3 would not	**4.** Again, the state of health of the chief executive might be very important to the company, but this would not be learned from the balance sheet. None of these facts could be expressed in _____ _____.	
4 monetary terms	**5.** The balance sheet, then, gives an _____ picture of the state of affairs of an enterprise because it is concerned only with things that can be expressed in _____ _____. This is one reason why the _____ _____ can never indicate how successful an enterprise will be in the future.	

CHECK	FRAME	YOUR ANSWER
5 incomplete monetary terms balance sheet	**6.** The balance sheet may show the resources available for the future, but the future success of the enterprise will depend on many factors including the product, the skill of _____ and staff, the activities of competitors, and general economic conditions.	
6 management	**7.** The first _____ of a balance sheet, then, is that it gives an incomplete picture of the state of affairs of the enterprise.	
7 limitation	**8.** A second limitation is that the monetary values shown on the balance sheet can never be completely exact and accurate. Consider the values given to the assets and those given to the liabilities. Which are more likely to be accurate and precise: the values given to the assets or to the liabilities?	
8 The values given to the liabilities	**9.** There will always be some uncertainty about the value of most of the _____ of an enterprise. The value given to them can never be exact.	
9 assets	**10.** Unsold stocks of finished products, for example, are part of the _____ assets. They are usually valued at cost or current market value, whichever is the _____.	
10 current lower	**11.** Suppose that unsold stocks are shown on a balance sheet at cost. Can the company be certain of getting exactly this amount of money when these stocks are eventually sold? _____.	

CHECK	FRAME	YOUR ANSWER

11
No

12. Again, it is very difficult to know what the fixed assets are worth. These are generally valued at _____, with an allowance for _____.

12
cost
depreciation

13. The figures entered against the fixed assets [are/are not] meant to represent resale value.

13
are not

14. A balance sheet, then, never gives a precisely accurate picture of the position in monetary terms because the values given to certain of the assets can never be _____.

14
exact

15. There is another reason why the picture that is given in monetary terms is never really accurate. Unless special inflation accounting techniques are adopted, the balance sheet assumes that the real value of money remains constant: in other words, then, a balance sheet assumes that the real value of money [changes/does not change].

15
does not change

16. Consider, for example, the long-term (fixed) liabilities. The figures on the balance sheet are the amounts borrowed: that is, the amounts that will eventually have to be repaid. But when the time comes for repayment, the real value of this money is likely to be [greater/less] than it was when the loan was first made.

16
less

17. The balance sheet, however, usually assumes that the _____ _____ of money remains constant.

CHECK	FRAME	YOUR ANSWER
7 real value	**18.** To sum up, one limitation of a balance sheet is that it can take into account only factors which can be expressed in _____ terms.	
18 monetary	**19.** A second limitation is that the values shown for some of the assets will never be _____.	
19 exact	**20.** A third limitation is that very often a balance sheet assumes that the real value of money remains _____.	
20 constant	**21.** In other words, we have to be extremely cautious about using the balance sheet as a guide to a company's _____ prospects.	
21 future	**22.** Even when we have a correctly drawn up, signed and audited balance sheet, where all concerned have a good reputation, we need to pay careful attention to other factors which cannot be reflected in the _____ _____ figures themselves.	
22 balance sheet	You have finally reached the end of the programme. Enter the usual data on the Progress Work Sheet, and reread the summary of this set before going on to the mini-test on this final chapter.	

MINI-TEST ON CHAPTER 7

Answer the questions below. When you have finished, check your answers, and fill in the Progress Work Sheet as usual.

1   It is often difficult to be certain that a balance sheet gives a true and reliable statement of a company's affairs. The general rule is: always be _____ about accepting a balance sheet without question. A balance sheet 11 months late is probably not _____.

2   To help you decide about the acceptability of a balance sheet, you can look at the balance sheet itself to see:

   (a) whether it shows the _____ of the company;

   (b) whether it gives the _____ of the balance sheet;

   (c) whether it is set out in such a way that it is possible to work out the values of the different classes of _____ and _____;

   (d) whether it indicates the basis of the _____ of the assets;

   (e) whether there is a certificate from a professionally qualified _____;

   (f) whether it is signed by one or more of the _____.

3   Other factors that you may have to consider are the reputation of the _____, of the _____, and of the _____ itself.

4   Above all, before accepting a balance sheet as a reliable statement, you have to be sure that it satisfies the _____ of the country.

5   The balance sheet gives an incomplete picture of a company's affairs because it includes only those items that can be ....

6   A second limitation is that the values shown on the balance sheet for some of the [assets/liabilities] will never be exact.

7   Thirdly, a balance sheet often assumes that the real value of money _____ _____.

8   On the basis of the balance sheet, can you judge how successful an enterprise will be in the future? _____.

9   The auditor should be p_____ qualified, i_____, and adequately p_____.

10 The key to understanding data on the balance sheet is to read the _____ to the financial statements.

Answers to mini-test on Chapter 7

1. cautious; reliable.

2. (a) name;
   (b) date;
   (c) assets; liabilities;
   (d) valuation;
   (e) auditor;
   (f) directors.

3. directors; auditor; company.

4. law.

5. expressed in monetary terms.

6. assets.

7. remains constant.

8. No.

9. professionally; independent; paid.

10. notes.

How did you get on?

6 or more correct	Excellent. Now read *all* the summaries *and* the glossary in Appendix B before trying the final quiz.
4 or 5 correct?	Read through the summaries of Sets 15 and 16 once more before going on to the final quiz.
Fewer than 4 correct?	Take a good break and then work through these last two sets once more.

FINAL QUIZ

The following questions test the knowledge you have acquired from the programme. Tick the most correct answer in each case.

1   It is impossible to estimate all the figures on a balance sheet absolutely accurately. Where there is uncertainty, the accountant drawing up the balance sheet must:
☐ (a) guess the correct values
☐ (b) ask the union for more information
☐ (c) use his judgement to estimate the figures as accurately as possible
☐ (d) leave the figures out, rather than put anything on the balance sheet which is not entirely accurate

2   A balance sheet is a statement of the position of an enterprise:
☐ (a) over a period of years
☐ (b) over a period of months
☐ (c) at a particular date
☐ (d) between two dates

3   A balance sheet gives two main groups of figures, the:
☐ (a) owners' equity and shareholders' funds;
☐ (b) assets and liabilities
☐ (c) profits and the total finance employed
☐ (d) big and small

4   A balance sheet cannot include information:
☐ (a) about the value of a company's assets
☐ (b) the extent of a company's liabilities
☐ (c) about money owed to shareholders
☐ (d) which cannot be expressed in monetary terms

5   Those items which a company owns and which consist of cash and things that will normally be converted into cash during the operating cycle of the business are known as:
☐ (a) current assets
☐ (b) current liabilities
☐ (c) fixed liabilities
☐ (d) fixed assets

6 Assets which can be quickly converted into cash are known as:
- ☐ *(a)* shareholders' funds
- ☐ *(b)* unstable
- ☐ *(c)* quick liabilities
- ☐ *(d)* quick assets

7 Land and buildings, plant and machinery, fixtures and fittings and motor vehicles all form part of a company's:
- ☐ *(a)* current assets
- ☐ *(b)* fixed assets
- ☐ *(c)* quick assets
- ☐ *(d)* liquid assets

8 Raw materials and work in progress form part of a company's:
- ☐ *(a)* current assets
- ☐ *(b)* fixed liabilities
- ☐ *(c)* quick assets
- ☐ *(d)* current liabilities

9 Which of the following do *not* form part of a company's assets?
- ☐ *(a)* stocks of unfinished goods
- ☐ *(b)* shareholders' funds
- ☐ *(c)* employee accounts
- ☐ *(d)* motor vehicles

10 Customers' accounts, employee accounts and other accounts outstanding are usually valued at:
- ☐ *(a)* the amount owed to the enterprise less provision for doubtful items
- ☐ *(b)* the amount owed to the enterprise less depreciation
- ☐ *(c)* cost + 10 per cent
- ☐ *(d)* cost or current market value, whichever is the lower

11 Which group of assets would normally be valued at cost or current market value, whichever is the lower, less provision for losses?
- ☐ *(a)* quick assets
- ☐ *(b)* fixed assets
- ☐ *(c)* plant and machinery
- ☐ *(d)* inventories

12 Which of the following assets are *not* normally valued at cost less depreciation?
☐ *(a)* motor vehicles
☐ *(b)* plant and machinery
☐ *(c)* buildings
☐ *(d)* investments

13 A business enterprise's short-term debts are shown on a balance sheet as:
☐ *(a)* quick liabilities
☐ *(b)* current liabilities
☐ *(c)* owners' equity
☐ *(d)* fixed liabilities

14 Fixed liabilities represent:
☐ *(a)* long-term finance
☐ *(b)* cheap finance
☐ *(c)* short-term finance
☐ *(d)* worries for management

15 Except for bank overdrafts, current liabilities generally:
☐ *(a)* should be reduced to a minimum
☐ *(b)* should not be more than half the shareholders' funds
☐ *(c)* should equal current assets
☐ *(d)* do not involve the payment of interest

16 The "outside liabilities" equal:
☐ *(a)* total finance − current liabilities
☐ *(b)* fixed assets + fixed liabilities
☐ *(c)* current liabilities + fixed liabilities
☐ *(d)* total liabilities − fixed liabilities

17 Which of the following is not part of the shareholders' funds?
☐ *(a)* marketable securities
☐ *(b)* issued capital
☐ *(c)* earned surplus
☐ *(d)* capital surplus

18 _____ _____ and _____ _____ are funds that have been retained in the company and not paid to shareholders.

☐ *(a)* cash in bank and employee accounts
☐ *(b)* fixed assets and current assets
☐ *(c)* earned surplus and capital surplus
☐ *(d)* current assets and issued capital

19 Profits made in the course of an enterprise's normal operation and retained in the business are called:

☐ *(a)* gross profit
☐ *(b)* earned surplus
☐ *(c)* operating profit
☐ *(d)* capital surplus

20 Profits arising from the sale of fixed assets are called:

☐ *(a)* operating profits;
☐ *(b)* non-operating profits
☐ *(c)* net profit before tax
☐ *(d)* depreciation

21 Which of the following represent a company's most permanent finance?

☐ *(a)* the fixed liabilities
☐ *(b)* shareholders' funds
☐ *(c)* goodwill
☐ *(d)* manager's savings for retirement

22 The amounts reflected on the balance sheet for earned surplus and capital surplus are the:

☐ *(a)* amounts accruing during the previous financial year
☐ *(b)* amounts accruing during the present financial year
☐ *(c)* cumulative totals at the date of the previous balance sheet
☐ *(d)* cumulative totals at the date of the balance sheet

23 Issued share capital will always be .... authorised capital.

☐ *(a)* less than or equal to
☐ *(b)* greater than
☐ *(c)* less than
☐ *(d)* greater than or equal to

24 Balance sheets always reflect:
☐ (a) a company's gross profit during a year's trading
☐ (b) the uses to which profits have been put
☐ (c) what a company owes and what it owns at a certain date
☐ (d) an enterprise's obligations for the future

25 Dividends are paid to shareholders out of the:
☐ (a) current assets
☐ (b) capital surplus
☐ (c) current liabilities
☐ (d) earned surplus

26 Fixed liabilities are usually:
☐ (a) short-term loans
☐ (b) long-term loans
☐ (c) bank overdrafts
☐ (d) hard to move about

27 If a business enterprise's total assets are greater than its outside liabilities, it is said to be:
☐ (a) liquid
☐ (b) highly geared
☐ (c) over-capitalised
☐ (d) solvent

28 An enterprise is said to be liquid if current assets:
☐ (a) are greater than they were on the previous balance sheet
☐ (b) are greater than fixed assets
☐ (c) exceed current liabilities
☐ (d) include a large inventory of milk products

29 If a company has fixed assets of 10,000 WCU, fixed liabilities of 5,000 WCU, current assets of 1,000 WCU and current liabilities of 500 WCU, working capital is:
☐ (a) 500 WCU
☐ (b) 5,000 WCU
☐ (c) 1,500 WCU
☐ (d) 15,000 WCU

30 If a company has a (high) gearing of 1 : 5, what proportion of the cost of assets is financed by shareholders' funds?

☐ *(a)* $\dfrac{1}{5}$

☐ *(b)* $\dfrac{1}{6}$

☐ *(c)* $\dfrac{4}{5}$

☐ *(d)* impossible to compute quickly

31 If a company has a (low) gearing of 1 : 1, then shareholders' funds are _____ _____ borrowed money.

☐ *(a)* greater than
☐ *(b)* less than or equal to
☐ *(c)* equal to
☐ *(d)* less than

32 A statement indicating where new money shown on a company's balance sheet has come from, and where money spent has gone to, is called a(n):

☐ *(a)* profit and loss account
☐ *(b)* income statement
☐ *(c)* earned surplus statement
☐ *(d)* sources and uses of funds statement

33 Which of the following items would *not* be included on the "sources" side of a funds flow statement?

☐ *(a)* new issued share capital
☐ *(b)* depreciation
☐ *(c)* new authorised share capital
☐ *(d)* new long-term loans

34 Which of the following items would be included on the "uses" side of a sources and uses of funds statement?

☐ *(a)* decrease in working capital
☐ *(b)* increase in authorised share capital
☐ *(c)* depreciation
☐ *(d)* increase in working capital

35 If a company's total assets were greatly reduced in value (because of a fire, for example), the company might find that it was no longer solvent. This would be the case if the company found that its _____ _____ now exceeded its total assets.

☐ (a) quick liabilities
☐ (b) outside liabilities
☐ (c) current liabilities
☐ (d) fixed liabilities

36 Which of the following statements is *not* true? The solvency ratio indicates the:

☐ (a) difference between total assets and outside liabilities, expressed as a percentage
☐ (b) relationship of shareholders' funds to total assets
☐ (c) relationship of shareholders' funds to total liabilities
☐ (d) relationship of long-term liabilities to short-term liabilities

37 Here is a table of assets and liabilities, expressed as percentages:

ASSETS	%	LIABILITIES	%
Current assets	49	Current liabilities	25
Fixed assets	51	Fixed liabilities	15
		Shareholders' funds	60
Total assets	100	Total liabilities	100

The solvency ratio in the above table is _____ per cent.

☐ (a) 25
☐ (b) 15
☐ (c) 60
☐ (d) impossible to work out without a micro-computer

38 If the solvency ratio has increased, this means that the excess of _____ assets over outside liabilities has increased.

☐ (a) total
☐ (b) current
☐ (c) fixed
☐ (d) outside

39 The ratio of current assets : current liabilities is the _____ ratio.
☐ *(a)* quick
☐ *(b)* solvency
☐ *(c)* current
☐ *(d)* turnover

40 Quick ratio = $\dfrac{\rule{3cm}{0.4pt}}{\text{current liabilities}}$: 1
☐ *(a)* mobile assets
☐ *(b)* fixed liabilities
☐ *(c)* quick assets
☐ *(d)* quick liabilities

41 The current ratio and the quick ratio are measures of:
☐ *(a)* solvency
☐ *(b)* liquidity
☐ *(c)* management pressures
☐ *(d)* gearing

42 Which of the following is the best indicator of how easily a company can meet its current liabilities at short notice?
☐ *(a)* current ratio
☐ *(b)* solvency ratio
☐ *(c)* net profit after tax
☐ *(d)* quick ratio

43 A company has current assets of 100 WCU, quick assets of 30 WCU and current liabilities of 150 WCU. The current ratio is:
☐ *(a)* 1.5 : 1
☐ *(b)* 0.67 : 1
☐ *(c)* 0.2 : 1
☐ *(d)* impossible to work out from the given figures

44 A company makes a gross profit of 100 WCU, has operating expenses of 33 WCU, has non-operating expenses of 17 WCU and pays tax on its year's profits of 13 WCU. The figure of 37 WCU represents:
☐ *(a)* operating profit
☐ *(b)* profit before tax

▶

☐ *(c)* net profit after tax

☐ *(d)* transfer to capital surplus

45 For the company referred to in question 44, profit before tax equals:

☐ *(a)* 50

☐ *(b)* 62

☐ *(c)* 66

☐ *(d)* 237

46 Which of the following are *not* deducted from the gross income from sales in calculating a company's operating profit?

☐ *(a)* cost of raw materials used in the goods sold

☐ *(b)* wages of workers producing the goods sold

☐ *(c)* wages of office staff handling accounts

☐ *(d)* interest on mortgage loan on factory premises

47 Any of the net profit after tax left over after payment of dividends is:

☐ *(a)* used to pay wages of any non-salaried staff employed

☐ *(b)* used to repay any long-term loans outstanding

☐ *(c)* included in earned surplus

☐ *(d)* included in capital surplus

48 Return on total investment and return on shareholders' funds are two useful measures of:

☐ *(a)* profitability

☐ *(b)* solvency

☐ *(c)* liquidity

☐ *(d)* a company's cost of borrowing

49 Return on total long-term investment is calculated by dividing profit before tax + interest on fixed liabilities by:

☐ *(a)* shareholders' funds + fixed liabilities

☐ *(b)* shareholders' funds + current liabilities

☐ *(c)* shareholders' funds + owners' equity

☐ *(d)* the outside liabilities

50 In calculating the return on total investment, "return" means:
□ *(a)* net profit after tax + interest on fixed liabilities
□ *(b)* profit before tax + interest on fixed liabilities
□ *(c)* profit before tax
□ *(d)* net profit after tax

51 If a company has shareholders' funds of 10,000 WCU, has fixed liabilities of 10,000 WCU, pays 1,000 WCU interest on fixed liabilities, makes a profit before tax of 3,000 WCU and pays 1,000 WCU in tax, return on shareholders' funds expressed as a percentage is:
□ *(a)* 10 per cent
□ *(b)* 15 per cent
□ *(c)* 30 per cent
□ *(d)* 20 per cent

52 Using the figures given in question 51, the return on total investment would be:
□ *(a)* 20 per cent
□ *(b)* 15 per cent
□ *(c)* 25 per cent
□ *(d)* 26.2317 per cent

53 In valuing an enterprise that is to be wound up, which of the following balance sheet figures is likely to be particularly misleading?
□ *(a)* current assets
□ *(b)* fixed assets
□ *(c)* current liabilities
□ *(d)* fixed liabilities

54 In valuing an enterprise that is to be sold as a going concern, which of the following figures will we not be able to get even from the most recent balance sheet?
□ *(a)* the value of the current assets
□ *(b)* future profits
□ *(c)* long-term loans outstanding
□ *(d)* trade accounts payable

55 Which of the following features is *not* essential on a well-drawn-up balance sheet?
- ☐ *(a)* the age of the accountant drawing up the balance sheet
- ☐ *(b)* the name of the company to which the balance sheet refers
- ☐ *(c)* the date of the balance sheet
- ☐ *(d)* separate totals for current and fixed assets and current and fixed liabilities

56 Before we can accept a balance sheet as a reliable and authentic statement, we would want to see that it:
- ☐ *(a)* has been signed by at least one of the directors and an external auditor
- ☐ *(b)* has been stamped by the tax authorities
- ☐ *(c)* is attached to the previous year's balance sheet
- ☐ *(d)* is accompanied by a sources and uses of funds statement

57 Some factors cannot be shown on a balance sheet but need to be taken into account in deciding whether or not a balance sheet gives a true and fair picture of a company's position. Which of the following is *not* such a factor?
- ☐ *(a)* the reputation of the company's auditor
- ☐ *(b)* compliance with the laws of the land
- ☐ *(c)* the reputation of the company and its directors
- ☐ *(d)* the true value of the fixed property of the company

58 In assessing a company's future potential, a balance sheet may *not* be sufficient because:
- ☐ *(a)* it does not show how the gross profit was calculated
- ☐ *(b)* it does not include an income statement
- ☐ *(c)* it reflects only items which can be expressed in monetary terms
- ☐ *(d)* fixed assets cannot be valued with absolute accuracy

59 Which of the following factors could be reflected on a company's balance sheet?
- ☐ *(a)* investment in new machinery and equipment
- ☐ *(b)* expected future technological developments
- ☐ *(c)* the state of the country's economy
- ☐ *(d)* the market value of its fixed assets

60 Which of the following is most correct?

☐ *(a)* a sources and uses of funds statement is necessary to determine a company's profitability

☐ *(b)* a balance sheet gives only a limited picture of the money an enterprise owes

☐ *(c)* fixed assets can be valued more accurately than current assets

☐ *(d)* a balance sheet is of limited value in predicting a company's future profitability.

Answers to the quiz

1 (c)	21 (b)	41 (b)
2 (c)	22 (d)	42 (d)
3 (b)	23 (a)	43 (b)
4 (d)	24 (c)	44 (c)
5 (a)	25 (d)	45 (a)
6 (d)	26 (b)	46 (d)
7 (b)	27 (d)	47 (c)
8 (a)	28 (c)	48 (a)
9 (b)	29 (a)	49 (a)
10 (a)	30 (b)	50 (b)
11 (d)	31 (c)	51 (d)
12 (d)	32 (d)	52 (a)
13 (b)	33 (c)	53 (b)
14 (a)	34 (d)	54 (b)
15 (d)	35 (b)	55 (a)
16 (c)	36 (d)	56 (a)
17 (a)	37 (c)	57 (d)
18 (c)	38 (a)	58 (c)
19 (b)	39 (c)	59 (a)
20 (b)	40 (c)	60 (d)

How did you do?

50 or more correct?	Excellent! Tomorrow you should start the technical note on inflation accounting.
40 to 49 correct?	Good. Now you should study the summaries again and try the quiz a second time.
Under 40?	You have probably learned quite a lot from the programme but, in order to benefit even more, perhaps you should wait for about a week and then try to do the whole programme again fairly quickly.

APPENDIX A

Technical note on inflation accounting

This technical note is designed to give you both a general idea of the basic concepts of inflation accounting and the opportunity to follow through, in examples A-H, some of the complexities of the computations required. The examples are more difficult than anything in the programme itself, but when you make use of what you have learned from the programme in your work, you may find it helpful to refer to this technical note.

First read the introductory section. Then study each example carefully. You will find an explanation of the figures in the explanatory notes.

Inflation

Inflation is a constant increase over time in the general level of prices which affects financial management decisions and accounting information. Accounting seeks to measure economic events and changes over time using monetary units, but during inflation the real value of such units constantly changes. As long as the rate of inflation is small, it is practical to ignore it; however, when the change becomes material (say, over 30 per cent per year) then accounting data from one year to the next are not comparable and can be misleading.

For instance, in Example B the profit and loss account shows a profit of 200 WCU which may have encouraged management to pay a dividend of 100 WCU for the year. However, when adjusted for inflation, the profit of 200 WCU becomes a loss of 83 WCU. Thus, the dividend of 100 WCU reduces the equity base (shareholders' funds) and the financial working capital of the company.

Problems

Inflation affects profitability and financing for both external published financial statements and internal financial reporting. While most accountants agree that inflation *must* be adjusted for, there is no agreement as to *how* it should be done or as to how valid and useful the results are. The two basic methods for accounting for inflation are: GPPA (General Purchasing Power Accounting) which uses one general government index of retail prices and CCA (Current Cost Accounting) which uses multiple price indices.

External financial reporting – GPPA method

For GPPA, all the items in a financial statement are calculated at a constant monetary value using a general price index provided by the government statistics office. Thus:

(a) the cost of fixed assets is adjusted for price changes from the date of purchase to the date of the balance sheet; and depreciation is calculated on the basis of the adjusted fixed asset cost;

(b) the opening and closing inventories are adjusted for price changes from the date of purchase and the cost of goods sold is adjusted accordingly;

(c) all profit and loss account items (other than cost of sales and depreciation above) are adjusted to current price levels;

(d) the net monetary working capital (debtors less creditors) is adjusted for price-level changes during the year.

The technique for these adjustments is objective but the general price index may not reflect the real changes in fixed assets or inventory costs; thus, GPPA adjustment may *not* reflect real profitability changes. Furthermore, the GPPA depreciation charges may *not* provide for replacement of fixed assets; accordingly, the financial statements produced may be misleading and of little value.

External financial reporting – CCA method

Under the CCA method, more specific estimates or price indices (computed by the government statistics office) are used for fixed assets and depreciation (towards replacement cost), inventories and cost of sales (towards changes in cost of materials). The technique of CCA does, therefore, reflect more specific price-level changes, but it is more subjective than the GPPA method and it has two major limitations:

(a) with technological change, fixed assets may *not* actually be replaced with identical equipment; thus the comparable replacement cost of old equipment may be irrelevant;

(b) loss of purchasing power of cash or near cash assets may, or may not, be included as a relevant adjustment.

Overall, the CCA method provides an indication of the cost of replacing fixed assets and inventories and is more relevant than the GPPA method. However, it is complex and difficult for non-accountants to understand.

External financial reporting practice

Some companies in countries with moderate inflation may revalue fixed assets to market value every five years; this increases assets and shareholders' funds (revaluation reserve) and reduces the profitability (due to increased depreciation charges). Some countries require inflation accounting under both GPPA and CCA methods to be shown as comparative data on normal financial statements.

Countries with high inflation (over 30 per cent per year) have introduced a variety of measures to reduce the tax burden on inflationary profits; however, where such tax laws differ significantly from generally accepted accounting principles, the value of the resulting profit and loss accounts and balance sheets is questionable.

Internal financial reporting

For internal financial reports where inflation is high (over 30 per cent per year), traditional standard costing and budgetary control systems become less useful because they are based on the false assumption of constant price levels. This affects many internal management decisions, particularly those based on evaluating profitability and the financing of working capital needs.

To deal with these problems, management needs to forecast systematically the long-term inflationary effects on inventories, fixed assets and depreciation, and other costs, as they affect profitability and financing. With high inflation, one year may be too long to maintain a single standard cost or budget level for the existing cost and budgetary control systems. Thus, it may be necessary to set up indices of price changes and to adjust the historical cost systems quarterly; with computerised accounting systems such complicated adjustments are feasible.

Conclusion

All companies *must* modify their traditional accounting and control techniques for high inflation (over 30 per cent per year) for both published financial statements and internal reporting, but only management can decide, by the usefulness of the result, what degree of complexity is justified.

A simplified example of the CCA (Current Cost Accounting) method of inflation accounting is given in Examples A to H. The example uses three different price indices: equipment, materials and the general price level. The GPPA (General Purchasing Power Accounting) method would be similar but would use only one general price index.

Example A

BALANCE SHEET

	1983 Historical cost		1983 Current cost	
ASSETS				
Fixed assets				
Cost/valuation		800	1 466	
Less: Accumulated depreciation		280	533	
		520	933	*(Ex. D)*
Current assets				
Cash	100		100	
Accounts receivable	500		500	
Inventory	400		500	*(Ex. H)*
	1 000		1 100	
Total assets		1 520	2 033	
LIABILITIES AND OWNERS' EQUITY (shareholders' funds)				
Current liabilities				
Accounts payable		400	400	
Fixed liabilities				
Long-term loan		520	520	
Owners' equity				
Capital	100		100	
Revaluation reserve	–		796	*(Note)*
Earned surplus	500		217	*(Ex. B)*
		600	1 113	
Total liabilities and owners' equity		1 520	2 033	

Explanatory notes

1. The balance sheet shows how the total assets increase from 1,520 to 2,033 because the company revalued fixed assets (520 to 933) and the inventory (400 to 500).
2. Earned surplus is reduced by 283 (Example B) (from 500 to 217) due to inflation adjustments.
3. Revaluation reserve is increased from 0 to 796 which consists of revalued fixed assets 413 (Example D) and inventory 100 (Example H), and profit and loss accounts adjustments 283 (Example G).

Example B

PROFIT AND LOSS ACCOUNT

	1983 *Historical cost*	1983 *Current cost*
Sales	2 500	2 500
Cost of sales	1 800	1 800
Gross profit	700	700
Operating expenses	300	300
Operating profit	400	400
Current cost accounting adjustments	–	283 *(Notes)*
Adjusted operating profit	400	117
Income tax	200	200
Net profit (loss)	200	(83)

STATEMENT OF EARNED SURPLUS

Opening balance	400	400
Net profit (loss)	200	(83)
	600	317
Less: Dividends paid	100	100
Closing balance	500	217 *(Ex. A)*

Explanatory notes

1. The profit and loss account shows how the profit of 200 is reduced to a loss of (83) by CCA adjustments:

Depreciation increase	133 *(Ex. D)*
Cost of sales increase	250 *(Ex. E)*
Monetary working capital increase	20 *(Ex. F)*
Subtotal	403
Less: Gearing adjustment-offset of inflationary losses by the debt: equity (long-term liabilities: shareholders' funds) structure	120 *(Ex. G)*
Net CCA adjustment (above)	283

2. The closing balance of the statement of earned surplus is reduced from 500 to 217 by the CCA adjustment of 283.

Example C

PRICE INDICES

	1982		1983	
	End of year	Average	End of year	Average
Equipment	250	200	400	300
Materials	200	200	500	400
General price level	270	100	300	200

Explanatory notes

1. These are price indices for equipment, materials and general price changes for the years 1982 and 1983 showing indices at the end of the year and average indices.

2. The indices come from government statistical reports and are used to adjust historical costs to current costs in Examples D to H.

3. Assumptions have been made so that only the end-of-year and average indices for each year are used. However, other more complex assumptions could be made.

Example D

ADJUSTMENT OF FIXED ASSETS

	Historical cost (HC)		Current cost (CC)	
	Cost	Accumulated depreciation	Cost	Accumulated depreciation
1982 Purchases	600	240	1 200	480
1983 Purchases	200	40	266	53
	800	280	1 466	533

Explanatory notes

1. The adjustment of fixed assets shows how the net book value of fixed assets 520 (800 less 280) is increased by revaluation of 413 to a net book value of 933 (1,466 – 533) (see 4 (c) below); it also shows how depreciation for the year is increased by 133 (293 – 160) (see 4 (d) below).
2. Depreciation is computed as 20 per cent per year.
3. The indices come from Example C.
4. The detailed adjustments for CCA are:
    (a) 1982 purchases — Cost:

    $$600 \text{ (HC)} \times \frac{400 \text{ (end 83)}}{200 \text{ (average 82)}} = 1\,200 \text{ (CC)}$$

    Accumulated depreciation:

    $$240 \text{ (HC)} \times \frac{400 \text{ (end 83)}}{200 \text{ (average 82)}} = 480 \text{ (CC)}$$

    (b) 1983 purchases — Cost:

    $$200 \text{ (HC)} \times \frac{400 \text{ (end 83)}}{300 \text{ (average 83)}} = 266 \text{ (CC)}$$

    Accumulated depreciation:

    $$40 \text{ (HC)} \times \frac{400 \text{ (end 83)}}{300 \text{ (average 83)}} = 53 \text{ (CC)}$$

    (c) Revaluation reserve:
Current cost net book value (1,466 – 533)	933 (CC)
Historical cost net book value (800 – 280)	520 (HC)
Revaluation reserve	413 (Ex. A)

    (d) Depreciation 1983:
Current cost: 20 per cent × 1,466	293 (CC)
Historical cost: 20 per cent × 800	160 (HC)
Depreciation increase	133 (Ex. B)

Example E

COST OF SALES ADJUSTMENT

Historical cost

Closing inventory	500 (HC)
Opening inventory (previous balance sheet)	<u>150</u> (HC)
Total increase (included in the calculation of the cost of sales)	<u><u>350</u></u> (HC)

Current cost at 1983 prices

Closing inventory $500 \times \dfrac{400 \text{ (average 83)}}{500 \text{ (end 83)}}$ 　　　400 (CC)

Opening inventory $150 \times \dfrac{400 \text{ (average 83)}}{200 \text{ (end 82)}}$ 　　　<u>300</u> (CC)

Cost of sales – volume increase	100
Cost of sales – price increase	250 *(Ex. B)*
Total increase (included in the calculation of the cost of sales)	<u><u>350</u></u>

Explanatory note

The cost of sales adjustment shows how the increase in inventory of 350 (500 – 150) is analysed into a volume increase of 100 and a price increase of 250. This price increase of 250 is due to inflation and therefore is adjusted on the income statement (Example B) as an inflationary effect.

Example F

MONETARY WORKING CAPITAL ADJUSTMENT (MWC)

Historical cost 1983

Accounts receivable	500 (HC)
Accounts payable	400 (HC)
Closing MWC	100
Opening MWC (Previous balance sheet)	50 (HC)
Total change	50

Current cost at 1983 prices

Closing MWC: $100 \times \dfrac{200 \text{ (average 83)}}{300 \text{ (end 83)}}$ 67 (CC)

Opening MWC: $50 \times \dfrac{200 \text{ (average 83)}}{270 \text{ (end 82)}}$ 37 (CC)

MWC volume increase	30
MWC price increase	20 *(Ex. B)*
Total change	50

Explanatory note

The monetary working capital adjustment shows how the net credit allowed has increased during the year to 100 (500 – 400) from 50 (on the previous balance sheet). This increase of 50 is analysed as a volume increase of 30 and a price increase of 20. The price increase of 20 is due to inflation and is adjusted on the profit and loss account (Example B) as an inflationary effect.

Example G

GEARING ADJUSTMENT

Net assets are financed by:

Liabilities

Long-term loan	520	*(Ex. A)*
Less: Cash	100	*(Ex. A)*
Net long-term liability financing	420	

Owners' equity (shareholders' funds)

Capital		100	*(Ex. A)*
Accumulated profit (before adjustment)		500	*(Ex. B)*
Revaluation reserves (before gearing adjustment):			
Fixed assets	413		
Inventory	100	513	*(Ex. A)*
Net long-term equity financing		1 113	

Proportion of inflationary changes financed by long-term liabilities (debt) rather than owners' equity:

$$\frac{420}{(1\,113 + 420)} = 27 \cdot 39 \text{ per cent} = \text{approximately} \quad \underline{\underline{30}} \text{ per cent}$$

Total inflationary adjustments	403	*(Ex. B)*
Gearing adjustment 30 per cent of 403 (approximately)	120	*(Ex. B)*
Net charge to income statement	283	*(Ex. B)*

Explanatory notes

1. The gearing adjustment shows how financing net assets with long-term debt (420) rather than equity (1,113) (i.e. with long-term liabilities rather than shareholders' funds) enables the company to pass on part (30 per cent) of the inflationary loss to long-term creditors.

2. In this case the gearing effect shows how the debt : equity (long-term liabilities : shareholders' funds) structure (420 : 1,113) of the company enables it to offset inflationary losses to the extent of about 30 per cent; thus, only 70 per cent of the 403 inflationary adjustments (depreciation 133, cost of sales 250, monetary working capital 20) is appropriate to the company and a gearing adjustment of 120 (30 per cent of 403) is deducted to show a net charge to the income statement of 283 (403 − 120).

Example H

INVENTORY ADJUSTMENT

Closing inventory	<u>400</u> *(Ex. A)*
Cost change from average 1983 to end 1983:	
Cost: $400 \times \dfrac{500 \text{ (end 83)}}{400 \text{ (average 83)}}$	500 *(Ex. A)*
Less: Historical cost (see above)	<u>400</u>
Revaluation reserve	<u>100</u> *(Ex. A)*

Explanatory note

The inventory adjustment shows how the 1983 closing inventory of 400 valued at average cost for the year is revalued with year-end indices by 100 (500 − 400), which is credited to the revaluation reserve (Example A).

APPENDIX B

GLOSSARY

The glossary includes terms used in this book and other accounting language which you might come across in the course of your work. Alternative expressions are given in parentheses after the main entry.

accounting the technique of preparing financial statements from bookkeeping records (based on accounting concepts such as those given below).

accounting concepts (accounting principles) practical rules which enable bookkeeping records of transactions to be converted into financial statements. The rules include concepts of cost, consistency, conservatism, comparability, going concern, accounting period, matching, profit realisation, materiality, etc.

accounts payable (creditors) money owed by a business. Accounts payable appear on the balance sheet under current liabilities.

accounting period the time interval from the date of one balance sheet to the next. The period of the profit and loss account (usually one year).

accounts receivable (see customers' accounts)

accrual (liability, creditor, payable, current liability) an accounting concept: income and expense for the accounting period, whether for cash or credit, must be included. Revenues must be matched with appropriate expenses to provide a meaningful net income figure for an accounting period, regardless of when cash may have been exchanged.

accumulated depreciation a total amount by which the original cost of a fixed asset shown on the balance sheet has been reduced to take into account deterioration and obsolescence. For example, consider a water works that costs 1 million WCU. Each year depreciation of 50,000 WCU is recorded against it. After five years its accumulated depreciation would be 5 x 50,000 WCU, or 250,000 WCU. The main purpose of depreciation is to help set prices so as to accumulate a fund that can be used to replace assets.

administrative expense cost of directing and controlling a business. This includes directors' fees, office salaries, office rent, lighting, heating, legal fees, auditor's fees, accounting services, etc. It is not a research, a manufacturing, a sales or a distribution expense.

ageing an analysis according to time elapsed after the billing date (or due date) to help management determine how to collect bills and to discipline customers.

amortisation (similar to depreciation) the process of writing off the cost of an intangible asset, such as a lease or patent, over its useful life. The accounting process for amortisation is similar to the process of depreciation for fixed assets.

appropriation account	(see statement of earned surplus)
asset	something owned by the business which has a measurable cost – fixed assets, current assets or other assets.
asset back-up	the realisable value of assets if the business is closed down; high value reduces the risk of loss to a new purchaser of an old business and thus the "downside risk" is low.
auditing	critical investigation of the accounting records and internal controls of an organisation. For many organisations it is a legal requirement that an audit be carried out by an independent accountant before the annual accounts of the organisation are issued.
auditor	accountant who carries out an audit.
authorised capital	(see capital authorised)
bad debt	debtor who fails to pay. The amount is written off as an expense in the profit and loss account.
balance sheet	a statement of the assets owned by a business and of how they are financed from liabilities and shareholders' funds. A balance sheet does not indicate the market value of the business.
bonds	(debentures) long-term loans, often secured on assets. These are not current liabilities.
book value	this can mean either *(a)* the value of assets in the books, the original cost of fixed assets minus their accumulated depreciation; or *(b)* the value of ordinary shares in the books (owners' equity less preference shares, divided by the number of ordinary shares).
buildings	these are classed as fixed assets, unless they are acquired for resale. Depreciation on buildings over their working life is charged as an expense in the profit and loss account. On a balance sheet they are valued at cost less depreciation, not at market value. They are sometimes revalued periodically. Land is not depreciated.
capital	this has several different meanings: *(a)* share capital; *(b)* shareholders' funds (net worth); *(c)* working capital; *(d)* fixed asset (as apart from small fixed assets which may be treated as expenses); *(e)* assets of the business.
capital authorised	the capital stock which a company is authorised to issue by law. It may be only partly issued for cash.
capital investment	a large investment in fixed or other long-term assets.
capital issued	the capital stock actually issued by a company. On the balance sheet it appears as part of the shareholders' funds. The price at which a share is first sold by a company (normally the nominal value plus share premium

less share discount). It may be issued as ordinary, preference or deferred shares.

capital reserve (see capital surplus)

capital stock (see share capital)

capital surplus capital profit which is not available for the payment of normal dividends.

cash the money asset of a business. It includes both cash in hand and cash in the bank. On the balance sheet cash appears as a current asset.

cash discount discount allowed to a customer for prompt payment of a debt, e.g. 2½ per cent discount for payment within ten days or net (no discount) for payment within one month.

cash flow cash receipts and cash payments over a given period – the key to liquidity.

chart of accounts a systematic list of all accounts for a concern. A chart of accounts with a description of their use and operation is a "manual", or a "book of accounts", which is a main feature of a "system of accounts".

claims claims against the assets of the business. These may be owners' or creditors' claims. Total claims equal total assets. Creditors' claims are called liabilities. Owners' claims are called shareholders' funds or owners' equity.

closing stock inventory at end of the accounting period. Part of the computation of the cost of goods sold.

comparability an accounting concept: financial statements should be prepared consistently so that the data are comparable.

company a legal entity, regulated by the Companies Act or the Corporation Act of the country concerned. A company may be "limited" or "unlimited".

consistency an accounting concept (see comparability).

conservatism an accounting concept: financial statements should avoid overstating the financial position. Profits are not usually recognised until they are realised. Losses are usually recognised as soon as they are known.

consolidated statements financial statements for a group of companies as a whole with transactions between subsidiary companies eliminated.

convention an assumption made in accounting. Many accounting concepts arise from assumptions that have proved to be practicable.

corporation tax tax on the profits of a company.

cost this has several meanings: (a) expenditure on a given thing; (b) to compute the cost of something; (c) a direct cost or an indirect cost (an indirect cost is an overhead).

cost concept	an accounting concept: assets are valued at cost not at market value. Exceptions: *(a)* fixed assets are valued at cost less depreciation; *(b)* current assets are normally valued at cost or market value, whichever is the lower.
cost of goods sold	(see cost of sales)
cost of sales	the cost of the goods actually sold during the accounting period. It excludes the cost of goods left unsold and all overheads except manufacturing overheads. The cost of sales appears in the profit and loss account. Sales less cost of sales equals gross profit.
creative accounting	(see manipulation) a polite term for manipulation.
creditor	(see accounts payable) a person or company who has supplied goods or services but who has not yet been paid for them.
credit transaction	a transaction which incurs (accrues) liability. No cash is paid or received until later.
cumulative preference shares	preference shares whose unpaid dividends accumulate until they are eventually paid by the company. Some preference shares are specifically non-cumulative.
current assets	assets which are normally realised in cash or used up in operations during one accounting period, normally one year. Current assets include cash, debtors, inventory and prepaid expenses but not fixed assets or other assets.
current liability	a liability due for payment within one operating period, normally one year. This does not include long-term liabilities or shareholders' funds.
current tax liability	current liability for income tax which is due within one year (see *also* future income tax liability).
current ratio	ratio of current assets divided by current liabilities. A measure of liquidity.
customers' accounts	(accounts receivable, debtors) money owed to a business. Customers' accounts appear on the balance sheet under current assets.
days of payables	(see ratios)
days of receivables	(see ratios)
debentures	(see bonds)
debt capacity	potential for borrowing more outside finance (related to gearing).
debtor	(see accounts receivable) someone who has received goods or services but has not yet paid for them.
deferred shares	(deferred stock) shares of a company ranking for dividend after preference and ordinary shares.

depreciation	the reduction of the original cost of a fixed asset by a certain amount each year over its working life. The amount is charged as an expense in the profit and loss account. Land does not depreciate (see *also* accumulated depreciation, depreciation expense, straight line depreciation and diminishing balance depreciation).
depreciation expense	depreciation (at cost) during the accounting period. This is not the same as accumulated depreciation except in the first year of the fixed asset.
diminishing balance depreciation	a method of depreciation which charges off the cost of a fixed asset by a level percentage of the reducing balance over its working life. The percentage remains the same but the depreciation charge decreases.
direct costs	costs conveniently associated with a unit of product. Normally direct labour, direct material, direct services (e.g. hire of equipment for one specific job). All other costs are indirect costs, known as overhead expenses. (Some cost accountants *also* use the term "direct" for specific costs, i.e. *overhead* expenses which are clearly identifiable with an overhead cost centre but *not* with a unit of product.)
director	the officer of a limited company. A member of the board of directors. Not a "partner".
discount	(see cash discount, trade discount)
dividends	that part of the net profit set aside for payment to shareholders; not an expense chargeable in the calculation of net profit in the profit and loss account; chargeable to the statement of earned surplus, it reduces the balance of earned surplus declared by directors on the balance sheet. It is not an automatic right of shareholders to receive dividends. A use of funds (see sources and uses of funds statement).
downside risk	risk of loss due to total business failure and subsequent liquidation of assets to pay creditors and owners (see asset back-up).
dual aspect	an accounting concept: two aspects of each transaction; the basis of double-entry bookkeeping; debit and credit.
earned surplus	(retained earnings, accumulated profit) the earned surplus available for the payment of dividends. Part of the shareholders' funds.
earnings	(income, profit, revenue)
entity	an accounting concept: financial statements are prepared for a specific entity. A shopkeeper, who personally owns his business premises, has three entities and rewards: ▶

Entity	business owner	*Reward*	profit
	landlord		rent
	employee		wages

equipment   a fixed asset if acquired for long-term use and not for resale. Equipment is recorded on the balance sheet at cost less depreciation, not at market value.

equity   money provided by the owners; any right or claim to assets. An equity holder may be a creditor, a part-owner or a proprietor.

expenditure   money paid for a cost, an expense, an asset or other purposes. An expenditure is charged against income in the period when that asset is consumed to help generate that income.

expense   expenditure properly chargeable in the profit and loss account. The amount used up during the accounting period. An indirect cost. A manufacturing, selling or administrative expense. Includes depreciation of fixed assets. Expenses are "matched" against revenues during the accounting period to compute the figure for profit. (Note: purchases of small, low-value fixed assets are often charged as expenses, in order to avoid depreciation calculations and to show a conservative financial position.)

face value   (nominal value, par value) this is not the book (shareholders' funds) value or the market value of shares.

financial ratios   (see ratios)

financial statements   the key statements are:

(*a*) the balance sheet;

(*b*) the profit and loss account;

(*c*) the statement of earned surplus;

(*d*) the sources and uses of funds statement;

(*e*) the auditor's certificate and notes to the financial statements.

fixed assets   assets such as land, plant and equipment acquired for long-term use in the business and not for resale. Such assets are depreciated over their working life. Fixed assets are recorded on the balance sheet at cost less depreciation, not at market value. Sometimes they are revalued periodically. Land is not depreciated.

fixed liabilities   (long-term liabilities) liabilities not due for payment within one year (e.g. bonds, debentures or loans). Holders are creditors and receive interest. They are not shareholders.

fixtures and fittings	miscellaneous office furniture and equipment. Such items are classed as fixed assets if they are acquired for use and not for resale.
funds flow statement	(see sources and uses of funds statement)
future tax liability	reserve for future income tax. Tax computed on the current year's profit not due for payment until a future date. This normally becomes the current tax liability in the following year.
gearing	the ratio of shareholders' funds to borrowed money (4 : 1 means 20 per cent borrowed (which is low); 1 : 4 means 80 per cent borrowed (which is high)). A "healthy" gearing ratio depends upon the industry averages.
general expense	an expense which is not a manufacturing, sales or administrative expense. General expenses are sometimes grouped with administrative expenses in the profit and loss account. They include auditor's fees, legal expenses, etc.
general reserve	part of the earned surplus set aside in the shareholders' funds section of the balance sheet. It is not distributed as dividends. It is not an asset and it is not cash. It is merely part of the shareholders' funds shown separately on the claims side of the balance sheet.
going concern	an accounting concept: all accounting reports and values assume that the business is continuing and is not about to be wound up (liquidated). In accounting, market values are therefore based upon those expected in the normal course of business.
goodwill	value of the name, reputation or other intangible assets of a business. In accounting, goodwill is only recorded (at cost) when it is purchased. It is not depreciated. It is often written off to nil. It is never valued at market price. Generally it is a hidden asset of the business.
gross profit	sales minus cost of sales. The profit computed before selling and administrative expenses, etc., have been deducted.
gross profit percentage	measure of profitability: $\dfrac{\text{gross profit}}{\text{net sales}} \times 100$ per cent.
income	(earnings, profit, revenue) this is sometimes used to mean sales and all forms of incoming benefits, not necessarily in cash. Money, or money equivalent, earned or accrued in an accounting period.
income statement	(see profit and loss account)
income tax liability	(see current tax liability *and* future tax liability)

inflation accounting   technique for adjusting normal (historical) financial statements according to changes in price levels (see Appendix A).

intangible asset   an asset which cannot be physically touched (may be shown separately or as part of the fixed assets). Goodwill and patents are examples of intangible assets.

investment   amount invested in stocks, shares, bonds, debentures or any asset (see *also* trade investments, marketable securities).

inventory   stock of goods (including supplies) available for resale. Inventory is valued at cost or market value, whichever is the lower, not at selling price. Increased by purchases. Decreased by cost of sales. On the balance sheet it appears as a current asset, not as a fixed asset.

issued capital   (see capital issued)

issue price of a share   the price at which stock is first sold by a company.

land   freehold or leasehold property owned by a business. Land is normally classed as a fixed asset. It is recorded at cost, and it is not depreciated. Sometimes land and buildings are revalued to market value. The difference between cost and revaluation increases fixed assets and increases capital surplus.

liability   an amount owed by one person or organisation to another.

limitations of accounting   financial statments show a limited picture of a business because: *(a)* some important facts cannot be stated in monetary terms; *(b)* accounting periods at fixed intervals involve uncertainty due to incomplete transactions; *(c)* financial statements depend on concepts; *(d)* accounting is not scientific, but depends upon judgement.

limited liability company   shareholders may risk losing all the money they have subscribed but they will not be liable for amounts beyond this. If a company could not meet its outside liabilities, the shareholders could not be called on to provide more money (in addition to what they had subscribed) to meet these outside claims. In other words, the shareholders' liability is limited. The limited liability company is one of the most common forms of business enterprise.

liquidation   the termination of a business whereby the assets are added up, the liabilities are paid, and the balance is paid to shareholders.

liquidity   the availability of cash or assets which can easily be turned into cash to pay liabilities. Liquidity is measured by the: ▶

$$\text{current ratio} = \frac{\text{current assets}}{\text{current liabilities}} : 1$$

or the

$$\text{quick ratio} = \frac{\text{quick assets}}{\text{current liabilities}} : 1.$$

long-term liabilities (see fixed liabilities)

loss (deficit) the opposite of profit or income. Excess of costs and expenses over income or sales. A loss reduces the shareholders' funds but may not affect the cash balance.

loss on disposal of fixed assets loss due to sale or disposal of fixed assets. Excess of fixed asset cost over accumulated depreciation, and scrap or sale proceeds. Treated as "other income and expense" in the profit and loss account. Significant losses or profits are sometimes charged to capital surplus.

machinery a fixed asset if acquired for use and not for resale. Machinery is valued at cost less depreciation. Machinery manufactured or acquired for resale is classed as inventory.

manipulation changes in values of assets and liabilities, using generally accepted accounting principles, to produce higher or lower profit levels (sometimes referred to as "creative accounting").

manufacturing expense overheads for manufacturing. Part of the cost of sales. It is not a sales or an administrative expense.

marketable securities quick assets; investments easily converted into cash.

materiality a key accounting concept whereby only "material" amounts are important, and "non-material" amounts may be ignored. The concept recognises that the balance sheet and associated financial statements are only reasonable estimates and not scientific facts.

matching an accounting concept: costs and revenues in the accounting period should be "matched" in order that the computed profit may be true and fair. Matching means "appropriate to" not "equal to".

money an accounting concept: financial statements are limited because they can only reveal facts about the business which can be expressed in monetary terms.

mortgage long-term loan normally secured on fixed assets, usually property. A mortgage is a long-term liability, not a current liability.

net this has two meanings: (*a*) figure after deduction (e.g. gross sales less sales returns equals net sales); (*b*) payment of the full amount due with no allowance for cash discount (e.g. 2½ per cent discount for payment within ten days, net for payment within 30 days).

net assets	assets less liabilities (see *also* return on investment, shareholders' funds).
net income	(*see* net profit)
net profit	(net income, net earnings) profit for the accounting period after income tax. The net profit increases shareholders' funds but does not necessarily affect the cash balance.
net profit percentages	measures of profitability:

(a) net profit to sales: $\dfrac{\text{net profit}}{\text{net sales}} \times 100$ per cent

(b) net profit to shareholders' funds (return on investment):

$$\frac{\text{net profit}}{\text{shareholders' funds}} \times 100 \text{ per cent.}$$

Note: return on investment may appear to be high if the assets on the balance sheet are significantly undervalued.

net worth	assets less liabilities. The shareholders' funds (or owners' equity). The balance sheet value of owners' claims based on accounting concepts. The net worth does not indicate the market value of a business.
nominal value	face (par) value of shares. Authorised and issued share capital on the balance sheet shows the nominal value of the shares separately from any premium or discount. The nominal value is not the book value or the market value of shares.
non-operating expenses	expenses not directly related to normal operations, e.g. loss on sale of fixed assets, interest paid, etc. Significant losses are sometimes charged to earned surplus or even to capital surplus.
non-operating income	income not arising from normal operations, e.g. profit on sale of fixed assets, dividends received, etc.
notes to the financial statements	notes attached to the balance sheet and profit and loss account which explain: *(a)* significant accounting adjustments; *(b)* information required by law, if not disclosed in the financial statements; *(c)* changes in the accounting concepts used to prepare the financial statements; *(d)* exceptions to consistency with previous figures; *(e)* contingent liabilities; *(f)* commitments. (Search here for evidence of manipulation.)
opening stock	inventory at the beginning of the accounting period.
operating expenses	all overheads of the business. Sometimes the term is restricted to mean only selling, administrative and general expenses.

operating profit	gross profit less operating expenses in the profit and loss account.
ordinary shares	part of the shareholders' funds on the balance sheet. Holders are entitled to dividends recommended by the directors. Not preference shares. Possible values: *(a)* face or nominal value; *(b)* market value; *(c)* issue price (including any premium); *(d)* book value (total shareholders' funds less the par value of preference shares) (*see also* deferred shares).
other assets	assets which are not fixed assets or current assets. Normally: goodwill, research expenditure carried forward, trade investments, etc. Other assets are valued at cost, not at market value, unless losses are exceptional.
other creditors	creditors or accruals for services. Not trade creditors for the purchase of material and supplies. Other creditors appear under current liabilities on the balance sheet.
overhead expense	(overhead) an indirect cost which may be fixed or variable according to the volume of production (see manufacturing, sales and administrative or general expenses).
owners' claims	(see shareholders' funds)
owners' equity	(see shareholders' funds)
par value	(see nominal value)
patent	legal right to exploit an invention. A patent is classed as an intangible asset on the balance sheet; it is recorded at cost less depreciation.
payable	(account payable, creditor)
plant	equipment and machinery. This is classed as a fixed asset if acquired for use and not for resale.
preference share	a share which entitles the holder to fixed dividends (only) in preference to the dividends for ordinary shares. On liquidation, holders are normally entitled only to the par value. Holders have no right to share in excess profits.
preference stock	preference shares in units.
prepaid expense	an expense paid in advance for more than one accounting period. Examples are prepaid rent or taxes and unexpired insurance premiums.
profit	(income, earnings) excess of sales over costs and expenses during an accounting period. Profit does not necessarily increase cash – it may be reflected in increased assets or decreased liabilities – but it increases owners' equity. The term "net profit" sometimes means profit less income tax.
profit after tax	net profit. Profit before tax, less income tax for the accounting period, in the profit and loss account.

profit before tax operating profit, less non-operating expenses, plus non-operating income, in the profit and loss account. It is not net profit.

profit and loss account (income statement) a statement showing sales, costs, expenses and profit for an accounting period.

profit and loss appropriation account (see statement of earned surplus)

profit realisation an accounting concept (see conservatism).

profitability (see net profit percentages)

provision this strictly means liability, but often has several different meanings: *(a)* reserve, e.g. future income tax liability; *(b)* accumulation, i.e. accumulated depreciation; *(c)* expense, e.g. depreciation expense; *(d)* accrual, e.g. accrued expense, liability.

published financial statements balance sheet, profit and loss account, statement of earned surplus, sources and uses of funds statement and notes to the financial statements, with comparative figures and notes disclosing the information required by law. They are less informative than internal statements (see *also* notes to the financial statements).

quick assets cash, call loans, marketable securities, a commodity immediately saleable, receivables. Quick assets are assets which can be made liquid in the immediate future, such as within a month.

quick liabilities that part of the current liabilities that is due to be paid soon (e.g. within one month); not normally shown separately on the balance sheet.

quick ratio ratio of quick assets to current liabilities. A measure of immediate liquidity (see gearing).

ratios useful indices of the financial health of an organisation. Healthy ratios are developed from industry averages according to the size of the organisation. Ratios include those for: *(a)* liquidity (quick ratio, current ratio, solvency (gearing) ratio); *(b)* activity (assets turnover (sales/assets), inventory turnover (cost of sales/inventory), days of receivables ((receivables/sales) × 365 days), days of payables (payables/cost of sales) × 365 days); *(c)* profitability (gross profit ratio, net profit ratio, return on investment ratio).

receivable (account receivable, debtor)

recognition of profit an accounting concept: profit (income) is not recognised and recorded until realised (in cash or debtors). By contrast, losses are recognised immediately they are known. Profit is normally recognised when goods are shipped to the customer, not when the order is received or when the customer pays for the goods.

reserve	this is a vague term. Strictly it means earned surplus (see also capital surplus, provision).
retained earnings	(see earned surplus)
retained profit	(see earned surplus)
return on investment	financial ratios are:

(a) return on shareholders' funds = $\dfrac{\text{net profit} \times 100}{\text{shareholders' funds}}$

(b) return on total investment =

$$\frac{\text{profit before tax} + \text{interest on fixed liabilities} \times 100}{\text{shareholders' funds} + \text{fixed liabilities}}$$

revaluation	sometimes fixed assets are revalued from cost to current values. The difference is credited to capital surplus.
revenue	(earnings, income, profit) sometimes it is also used to mean sales.
sale	the price for which goods are sold; the total of amounts sold. A sale is normally recognised when goods are shipped to the customer.
sales discount	trade or cash discount on sales.
sales expense	cost of promoting sales and retaining custom. Such an expense is an indirect cost, an overhead expense. It is not a manufacturing, administrative or general expense. Sales expenses include advertising, sales publications, sales salaries, travelling expenses, depreciation of cars used by salesmen, etc.
security	(collateral) an asset pledged against a liability. Assets claimable by some creditors in priority to others.
share	a document certifying ownership of shares in a company. Share capital. Part of shareholders' funds.
share capital	(capital stock) part of shareholders' funds. Money put into a business by the owners. Ordinary, preference or deferred shares.
shareholder	owner of part of the share capital and shareholders' funds.
shareholders' funds	(owners' equity, owners' claims) the amount due to owners of the business. Shareholders' funds are increased by profits and reduced by losses and dividends. (Assets less liabilities equals shareholders' funds.)
share premium	(stock premium) excess of original sales price of a share over its face or par or nominal value.
solvency	a situation where there are sufficient total assets to meet the outside liabilities.

solvency ratio

this is related to the gearing ratio; it is expressed as a percentage and it shows the degree of risk. It may be measured in two ways:

$$(a) \ \frac{\text{shareholders' funds}}{\text{total assets}} \times 100 \text{ per cent}$$

$$(b) \ \frac{\text{shareholders' funds}}{\text{total assets less current liabilities}} \times 100 \text{ per cent.}$$

The first considers the relationship of shareholders' funds to total liabilities. The second relates shareholders' funds to long-term liabilities only.

sources and uses of funds statement

(sources and application of funds statement, funds flow statement) this statement shows the key financial management decisions for the accounting period by indicating the sources of funds and the uses to which the funds have been put. Sources are net profit plus depreciation, new loans and new capital issued. Uses are dividends, the purchase of fixed assets and increase in working capital.

statement of earned surplus

(profit and loss appropriation account, statement of accumulated profit, statement of retained earnings) a statement showing the earned surplus brought forward, plus net profit, less dividends, to give the earned surplus to be carried forward to the next year on the balance sheet.

stock

usually means capital stock or shares (note that, in Europe and in the retail trades, stock is also used to mean inventory).

stockholder

(shareholder)

straight line depreciation

depreciation method charging off the cost of a fixed asset equally over the years of its working life (see *also* depreciation, diminishing line depreciation).

subsidiary

a company, of which the majority of shares are owned by another organisation. The latter is the parent company.

tangible asset

an asset which can be physically identified or touched.

trade creditor

(see accounts payable, creditor)

trade discount

deduction from the selling price of an invoice because the buyer is in the same trade as the seller. Not a cash discount.

trade investment

investment in shares or debentures of another company in the same trade or industry. This is a long-term investment, not a marketable security. It is listed under "other assets" on the balance sheet. It is valued at cost, unless there is a substantial loss.

transaction	a business event recorded in the accounts; a change in two items on the balance sheet (a cash or a credit transaction). A transaction may be a sale, a purchase, a cash receipt, a cash payment or an accounting adjustment. Translated into debits and credits in the bookkeeping records.
true and fair	an accounting concept: the balance sheet and the profit and loss account show a "true and fair view" of the business, in accordance with generally accepted accounting principles.
uncertainty	limitation of accounting. Uncertainty at the end of each accounting period makes it difficult to determine the "true and fair" position. Uncertainty arises from: *(a)* incomplete transactions; *(b)* the market value of inventory; *(c)* the working life of fixed assets for depreciation calculations; and *(d)* the realisable values of assets; and *(e)* contingent liabilities not yet known or calculable.
unpaid dividends	dividends declared as due to shareholders but not yet paid in cash. These are shown as current liabilities on the balance sheet. They are deducted from earned surplus in the shareholders' funds.
value	this has several meanings: *(a)* accounting value – value according to accounting concepts, appropriate to the particular asset. Fixed assets are valued at cost less depreciation. Current assets are generally valued at cost or market value, whichever is the lower; *(b)* market value – realisable value of inventory in the normal course of business (not on liquidation); and *(c)* real value – not known in accounting.
working capital	(net working capital) current assets less current liabilities. Working capital is not the same as capital. "Monetary" working capital refers only to cash, receivables and payables.
working capital ratio	(see current ratio)
work in progress	work partially completed. Part of inventory, stock. Valued at manufacturing cost or market value, whichever is the lower.

OTHER ILO PUBLICATIONS

Creating a market. An ILO programmed book

"This course deals with the planning and commercial aspects of marketing, mainly in the consumer goods industries ... It is as lucid and logical an introduction to the often complicated marketing process as can be found. Every student aiming for a Business and Industry Management Diploma should regard this manual as a must." (*Management*, Auckland)

"The reviewer can do nothing better than strongly advise the reader to read the book carefully and go through the exercises. This will be a most profitable venture." (*Social Action*, New Delhi)

ISBN 92-2-100082-6

Promoting sales: A systematic approach to Benefit Selling.
An ILO programmed book.
By Owen Dibbs and Patricia Pereira

The Benefit Selling method of marketing goods and services and selling ideas has proved its fundamental worth time and time again. This book goes further than many other courses on Benefit Selling: it develops a new, simple and practical approach to Benefit Analysis which enables the reader to master Benefit Selling rapidly and surely, showing what to do, how to do it and why the method suggested is so successful.

ISBN 92-2-101393-6

Economics. A workers' education manual

One of the oldest mottoes of the workers' education movement is "Knowledge is Power". For trade unionists, an understanding of economics is one of the essential forms of knowledge. This manual is published in the belief that the first step in introducing workers to the study of the subject of economics must be to prove that it is of direct relevance to their working lives, and one which as trade unionists they would do well to investigate. The manual therefore starts with a consideration of the workers' standard of living, in terms of jobs, pay, prices and social benefits, and then moves on to the subject of workers and enterprises (types of enterprise, prices and markets, production, location of industry, investment, wage determination and workers' access to management information), before approaching what may appear to be the more remote subject of the national and international framework within which workers and employers earn their living. The book is written, as far as possible, in everyday language, and where abstract economic terms are used their sense is clearly explained in the text and in an appended glossary of common economic terms.

ISBN 92-2-103265-5

Wages. A workers' education manual

The more trade union leaders and members know about what determines wage levels, the causes of differences between wages in various occupations, industries and regions, and the methods of wage payment (time-rates, piece-rates and bonuses), the more effective will their action be in securing improvements, removing anomalies that are unjustifiable and establishing proper wage structures.

This volume, consisting of 16 lessons, has been written mainly for use in study courses attended by trade union members and other workers so that they may gain a clear understanding of the issues involved. This is not a treatise on economics but a practical tool that can be adapted to the widely varying circumstances characteristic of workers' education.